CW00952253

This book is dedicated to our beloved residents,
both those living and those who have passed away.
We want to thank you for being a constant source of
inspiration and encouragement to us. Thank you for
the privilege of worshipping with you, for sharing in
your journeys of faith and for all you have taught us
about living older age well.

Who are we?

Meet the authors......

Lindsay Pelloquin is the Lead Chaplain of The Gift of Years Rugby, an ecumenical chaplaincy team providing pastoral and spiritual care to older people living in residential care homes in Rugby. This team is sponsored by the local churches as part of Rugby Revive.

www.thegiftofyearsrugby.com

The Gift of Years Rugby is affiliated to BRF's Anna Chaplaincy which is a national network of ecumenical, community-based chaplains in ministry to older people.

www.annachaplaincy.org.uk

In creating this resource for those leading worship in care homes, Lindsay has drawn on her own experience of leading worship over many years in a variety of different residential settings.

And....

Jaye Keightley has worked in a residential care home since 2008, where he is responsible for the development of a social care service. He has assisted with music for worship, the use of technology in worship and has been involved in creating resources for worship in care settings.

Jaye has worked freelance as a trainer for The Gift of Years Rugby and has been involved in training chaplains and volunteers who serve in care homes as part of a team.

The Life Worth Living concept has been inspired by our experience of working together in partnership, to help older people and those with dementia to live meaningful lives in care homes, through the provision of spiritual and social care resources. It is our aim to help residents to not just *exist* in a care home, but to really *live* fulfilling lives, and to foster a sense of belonging through creating supportive and stimulating communities. Together we have witnessed an inner awakening of residents and a desire to truly live!

We hope that this book will inspire you to create services of worship which enable residents to participate and to experience the presence of the Lord, and which bring colour and joy and life to the homes in which they live.

For more information about the training materials and our spiritual and social care resources for care homes please contact us at.....

email: giftofyearsrugby@outlook.com
phone: **07842 993847**

Copyright Guidelines

The authors have created a downloadable resource to accompany this book
Services can be downloaded by clicking on the link:
https://www.thegiftofyearsrugby.com/celebrating-the-seasons

Password is DQQpJdmcP

You only have permission to....

- Copy for **your own use** the services, talks and prayers in this book
- Change or adapt the services for your own situation
- Take ideas from the book and then create your own services

You must ask permission from the authors to....

- Copy any other material from the book eg. text and photographs

You **do not** have permission to....

- Reproduce or transmit in any form or by any means electronic or mechanical, including photocopying, recording, or by any information storage and retrieval system in order to **share content with other parties. Worship leaders should purchase their own copies of Celebrating the Seasons.**
- Copy the pictures by The Benedictine Nuns of Turvey Abbey
  Please purchase these pictures from McCrimmons or St. Paul's Media stores - details in the **Resources for worship** section at the back of the book.

Copyright © Lindsay Pelloquin & Jaye Keightley 2022
First Published 2022

Lindsay Pelloquin & Jaye Keightley have asserted their right to be identified as the authors of this work in accordance with the Copyright, Designs and Printing Act, 1988
Published by The Paul Thomas Group, Rugby, CV21 4NY
All rights reserved. No part of this publication may de reproduced, stored in a retrieval system, or transmitted in any form or by any means, electronic, mechanical, photocopying, recording or otherwise, without prior permission of the publisher.
ISBN 978-1-7398720-0-7
Printed in the UK by Lightning Source UK Ltd. Milton Keynes, MK11 3LW

Contents

Chapter 10: Ordinary Time   Page 211-212

Resources for worship   Page 297-298

Acknowledgements

Training Resources - by the same authors

Introduction

Welcome to Celebrating the Seasons in Residential Care Homes.

This book is intended to be a resource for chaplains, ministers and lay people who are involved in leading services of worship in care homes. We hope that it will inspire you to create services which we have termed 'Three dimensional worship that engages the senses and emotions.' (See pages 3-9 for a fuller explanation of what we mean.) The orders of service in this book have all been used before in a variety of residential settings and can be used as they are or adapted and changed for your own situation. There are many photographs illustrating how we have celebrated the seasons which we hope will stimulate your own ideas and creativity. The services have been formatted so that they can be downloaded from our website and copied as they are for your residents to use. Please follow the copyright guidelines regarding permission to copy the material in this book. The talks and prayers in this book are designed to stimulate your own reflections and rather than reading them straight from the book we hope that you will adapt them and make them your own. These services have been created for mixed congregations of people with and without dementia. For congregations of people who do not have dementia you may want to develop the themes more and make the talks a little longer. For congregations where people's dementia is moderate to advanced you may want to simplify the services further and sing hymns, talk about the pictures and have a short prayer.

Who are your congregation?

Many of you reading this book will be working with people who are living in what is now called the fourth age of life. That is, they are aged 85-100 years old. They are living in residential care because they are physically frail and can no longer manage at home, they have medical needs or physical disabilities which mean that they need nursing care or they are living with dementia.

This generation went to church and Sunday School when they were young and so they have some understanding of Christianity. They know some Bible stories and some hymns. Generally they know how to conduct themselves in a service of worship.

In the care homes in which we have worked, we have found that usually there are a small number of residents who have been regular church-goers and whose faith is very important to them. These residents usually really want to attend the service in the care home and do draw great strength and comfort from it. Often they have missed going to church if they have no longer been able to go and the service in the care home becomes church for them. These people will often enjoy being able to play a part in the service for example reading from the Bible, saying a prayer, helping to lead the singing, welcoming, serving drinks afterwards.

We have also found that there is a larger number of residents who have not gone to church regularly in their lives or really practised their faith, but a little seed of faith was planted in them when they were young which has been lying dormant within them. They would say that they believe in God and that they pray some-times. Now they are living in a care home where there is a service happening regularly and they decide to come along, or perhaps are encouraged to come by another resident or member of staff. When they come they find they can remember the hymns and enjoy singing them again. All sorts of memories are being triggered of singing hymns at school or Sunday School. They can remember Sunday School outings and Harvest Festivals. Often these memories are happy and bring comfort. Gradually over time the little seed that was planted long ago begins to be watered and starts to grow.

The services in this book have been designed to tell the whole story of Jesus. His birth, his life, his stories, his teaching, his death, his resurrection, his ascension and his constant presence with us through his Spirit. There are challenges to respond to his call 'Follow me'. There are opportunities to really encounter him and reflections on how they might live for him in the care home where they now dwell. There are moments to grapple with some of the more difficult questions of life and death that face older people.

It is our sincere prayer that the material in this book will help people to meet Jesus, to activate seeds of faith, and enable people to grow in their love of God and in so doing experience hope and his strength, comfort and peace.

The chapter: Worshipping in a care home offers advice on how to manage services of worship in care home settings where the environment is very different from worshipping in a church building. It also looks at how to make services accessible to people with complex needs which means that they now may not be able to see or hear very well, they may no longer be able to read, or concentrate for very long or process words. The services we are used to in church have lots of words - liturgies, readings, sermons, prayers, but many of our residents can no longer listen, process and understand words so we must find other ways of helping people to experience the presence of the Lord.

We hope that you will enjoy exploring three dimensional worship with us.....

Please feel free to contact us to share your ideas and experiences with us.

Lindsay and Jaye

WORSHIPPING IN A CARE HOME

Worshipping in a Care Home

Introduction

Leading worship in a care home is very different from leading worship in a church. There are various factors to take into account when you are preparing to hold a service.

Your congregation will have a variety of complex needs including sight loss and hearing impairment, physical disability and different forms and degrees of dementia. Relating to people with these needs and enabling them to engage in worship is a real challenge.

You are not meeting in a church which is a purpose built, sacred space for worship, but you are in a care home where ordinary daily life is happening all around you. It can be noisy and distracting for the residents and the care staff may not really understand why you are there or what support you need to make a service happen.

When we meet together at church everybody has chosen to be there, whereas in a care home not everyone who lives there will want to attend worship. Chaplains and worship leaders should be sensitive to residents' different needs, and attending services, just like any other activity, should not be imposed on anyone who would not want to be there.

Setting up the room for worship

Preparing the room is a very important aspect of leading worship in a care home. If possible, use a room that is not attached to a kitchen or dining room area and where it is possible to minimize distractions and to be quiet. However it may be that the only possible place for worship is a communal lounge. If so, check that residents who are sitting in the room want to attend worship, and if not, give them the option of moving to an alternative lounge or to another room.

Set up the room to look like a chapel, and create the right atmosphere for worship by turning off the television and play music or hymns in the back-ground as people arrive. It helps if you create a visual display at the front, with a table and items such as a cross, flowers, candles, Bible etc. You may want to use liturgical colours to help orientate people to the seasons of the year. You may want to have a picture or something visual to look at which indicates the theme of the service. Arrange curtains and lighting to enable people to see, and use microphones and loop systems so people can hear.

It is really important to greet people warmly by name when they arrive and seat them carefully to maximise their engagement. Seat people who have visual impairment, hearing loss or difficulties concentrating near to the front. Seat people with advanced dementia next to a volunteer who can help them to concentrate and participate.

Use large bold print, light-weight hymn books with portions of the service inside the front and back covers. Or use a simple printed order of service. Space the print so that it is easier to see and to read. For special occasions such as carol services, it can help to make your own booklets with songs and prayers all in the right order. Only give people one book or one sheet as they will become confused if given lots of paper or different books to hold. Ideally print out the hymns on different coloured paper and staple them together in the right order, so they can be easily recognised by people of all abilities. Ask volunteers to assist residents to find pages in the hymn books. Some people with dementia can read a simple order of service or the words of a hymn if a volunteer will sit next to them and place a finger under each word to help them to know where they are on the page.

A lot of flexibility is required when leading worship in a care home, but try to gather all the residents that would like to attend worship and then begin together. It can be very distracting for everyone if residents are brought in late or if there is a lot of coming and going and manoeuvring of people in wheelchairs during the service. Try to have everyone settled before you begin. However, be mindful of the place you are in. There may well be emergencies at times that staff members have to deal with, so always make sure that there is a clear point of access for all, to enable individuals to leave the room quickly should they need to.

Volunteer Support

Volunteers have an important role to play in helping worship in care homes to go smoothly, and to be beneficial to residents. Volunteers can help to set the room up in the way that has been described. Before the service they can go around the care home reminding the staff that the service will be happening. They can invite residents to the service, and let the staff know who would like to come. They can accompany ambulant residents to the service. Volunteers can sit among the residents, supporting those who need help and reassurance. They can help to create the right atmosphere by joining in with the hymns, prayers and responses. At the end of the service they can help to serve coffee and chat to residents.

Putting together a service of worship

When creating an order of service it helps to remember why you are there. You are there to help the elderly residents to, in some way, connect with God and to experience his presence. This requires an approach that involves both thinking inside and outside of the box.

4

Choose familiar resources

You need to think inside the box by choosing resources which will help your congregation to be able to participate in worship as fully as possible. This means using resources that residents can relate to and are familiar with, such as well-known hymns, songs and prayers and familiar liturgies. These hymns and prayers are in the long-term memory, which can often be accessed even by people with advanced dementia and will enable them to feel part of what is going on. Often familiar hymns and prayers have a comforting and

calming effect on people who feel confused and disorientated. They can also have the effect of stimulating other parts of the long term memory, and then more of the person inside is awakened and revealed. They may begin to tell you about the times and places where they have sung these hymns and memories of weddings, Sunday School and special occasions may be shared. Having a printed order of service really helps some people to follow the service, but it is important to use bold, large print and to have the words spaced on the page so people can see them. Using a set, familiar, structure which includes familiar prayers such as the Lord's Prayer and the Grace, enables residents to participate. Services should be about half an hour in length.

Making worship a three dimensional experience that engages the senses and emotions.

It is not sufficient to do a shortened version of a church service. Residents who are no longer able to read or to communicate with coherent speech and those whose minds are muddled and disorientated will have great difficulty engaging with a very word - based service. They will have difficulty holding the thread of long readings, talks and prayers and will tend to switch off or go to sleep or may even become disruptive. Thinking outside of the box means that we have to carefully consider how we will facilitate worship in a way that enables people who are cognitively impaired to actively engage and participate. We are more than just minds, and words are not enough.

The Church's Year

Advent, Christmas, Lent, Easter, Pentecost, Harvest and Remembrance.

Following the liturgical year is a great resource for worship in care homes. Life in a care home can be a very monotonous experience for elderly residents. Often every day is the same and follows a set routine and structure. The only thing that changes is the menu. Some residents do not know what time of year it is. Following the liturgical year introduces colour and variety and gives a reason and opportunity to celebrate. There are special activities, particular music, different traditions and a variety of special food associated with each season. Each season has its own particular mood. When following the liturgical year the mundane-ness of life is broken up and there are special events to plan for and times of celebration to enjoy. Sharing in these times and seasons helps to foster a sense of community and belonging as well as stimulating the memory, senses and emotions.

Stimulating the senses

Sight

Use colours to correspond with the liturgical year and the seasons of nature. Use pictures and other visual aids to illustrate the theme of the service. Short You Tube films or pictures on PowerPoint can sometimes be effective if used in the right way. Vases of flowers and colourful displays of fruit and vegetables at harvest time, candles around Christmas time all help to orientate residents as to the season of the year.

Sound

Music is a powerful resource, choose carefully to create the right kind of mood or atmosphere, to reinforce the theme of the service and help to orientate people to the season of the year. Music, songs and hymns can awaken people with dementia in a wonderful way, by stimulating the memory and can help to maintain language. The words of scripture that are hidden in hymns remain in the memory and can be recited and can help people to feel connected with God and with their faith. Music provides an outlet for emotion when a person cannot communicate in words how they feel. Some people who can no longer

communicate coherently with words can still sing hymns. This brings them pleasure and enables them to participate and to feel part of what is going on. Most people have certain music which is particularly special to them and this can be selected to awaken them and enable them to connect with the worship and with God.

Touch

Touch is a powerful resource which should be used sensitively and appropriately. Gestures such as sharing the Peace, placing a cross on the forehead, holding a hand or placing a hand on someone's head in blessing can bring forth a response even from those with advanced dementia. Joining hands to say the Grace to one another at the end of the service helps people to notice one another and fosters a feeling of belonging and community.

Smell

The smell of flowers for Mothering Sunday, candles during Advent, greenery at Christmas, the smell of bread baking and food at Harvest are all evocative of times and seasons in our lives and act as powerful memory joggers which can stimulate reminiscence.

Taste

The taste of bread and wine in the communion is a special reminder of the presence of Jesus with us when we worship together. Residents can continue receiving communion for as long as they are able. If they come to the point where they no longer know what it means, Jesus is still able to bless them and be close to them as they receive.

Mood and atmosphere

Each season of the year has its own mood and atmosphere. Celebrating the seasons and feeling these different moods breaks up the monotony of life in a care home and encourages the expression of emotion.

Easter Garden

Garden Tomb

Recommended Order of Service

Where your congregation is mainly one particular denomination it will be appropriate to use the liturgy or order of service that they are familiar with. However in most care homes there will be residents from a variety of church backgrounds living together. In this case the following simple, ecumenical order of service is recommended.

Welcome and Introduction

Open the service by welcoming everyone warmly and orientating them to what will be happening next eg.
"Good morning everyone, and welcome to our Wednesday morning service."

If you notice any new residents in the room or any relatives, make a point of welcoming them. Welcome volunteers and helpers.

Introduce yourself. Don't assume that they know who you are. Tell them which church you belong to and bring them greetings from that church.

Introduce the theme of the service to help set the scene for the residents. Refer to any pictures or visual things that you have brought with you.

A moment's silence

Often it can be quite a hectic time, gathering the residents and getting everyone settled, so a moment's silence enables everyone to collect their thoughts, quieten their hearts and become aware of the presence of the Lord in the room.

Opening responses

Using an opening response is a good way to all begin together. It invites the residents to be actively engaged and to participate. You can teach the response and have a little practice and then do it for real.

Hymn

Choose hymns which reinforce the theme of the service and which help to create the kind of mood and atmosphere that you want.

Confession

This gives time in the service for people to put themselves right with God and with one another.

Bible Reading

Choose a reading which reinforces the theme of the service or is appropriate for the season of the year. If possible use well known passages and stories that will be familiar and keep it short, because some residents will not be able to concentrate and will lose the thread if it is too long.

Talk

Keep it short – no more than 5 minutes. Use pictures or visual things to help engage people. Have only one theme, one point you want to make and keep to subjects that are simple and concrete, rather than those requiring abstract thinking. Talk about things that people can relate to, things that will stimulate memory. Focus on Jesus and on gospel stories. Bring a message of Good News, of hope and return often to themes about God's love, his presence with us in all we are going through. Sometimes bring a little challenge about living our faith in the care home setting. Asking a question or inviting a response from residents can help to keep them engaged.

Hymn

Choose a hymn to reinforce the theme of the talk or to continue on from it. It can help to read the first verse of the hymn, or any phrases which relate to your talk.

Prayers

Keep prayers short and relevant to the lives of the residents. Pray for them and their families and about things that matter to them. Pray for the world, but don't go into a lot of detail about all the violence etc. or about complex political situations. Pray for the staff and the home. In between each short prayer have a response such as, Lord in your mercy…… hear our prayer. This helps residents to stay with the prayers. If prayers are too long and not broken up, there is a risk that residents will go to sleep! Draw all the prayers together in the words of the Lord's Prayer.

Hymn

Continue the theme of the service.

Blessing

The Grace

Finish the service by joining hands (optional) and saying the Grace to one another. This helps people to notice one another and to feel part of a community.

Coffee and Fellowship

After the service encourage residents to stay for refreshments. If possible seat them in groups around coffee tables so they can talk to one another. Volunteers can help by sitting in these groups to facilitate conversation and help residents to get to know each other.

Resident participation

Encourage more able residents to take part in the service or to take on new roles such as greeting people as they arrive, helping with readings and prayers or serving drinks and biscuits at the end. In allocating these new roles to residents, you are helping them to feel useful and are giving them the opportunity to show they are still able to contribute.

ADVENT

Introduction

Anyone working in residential care will know that Christmas comes very early in care homes. Decorations are brought out and often by the end of November or beginning of December the whole home is garlanded in tinsel and there are Christmas trees, lights and images of Santa everywhere. Nostalgic Christmas songs play in the background throughout the day and local school children and community choirs come to sing carols. Residents can be in no doubt that Christmas is coming or could be today! But what about the season of Advent? Perhaps like the world outside the care home, Advent has been swallowed up by all the practical preparations for Christmas and its meaning somehow lost amidst the hustle and bustle and noise.

The season of Advent is however so meaningful for residents who are nearing the end of their lives. Advent is a time of preparation and waiting in anticipation and hope for the coming of Jesus. In Advent we prepare our hearts to welcome Jesus. We prepare to celebrate his birth in Bethlehem. We prepare for his second coming at the end of time. But also, Advent is a time to help our residents to prepare themselves to meet Jesus at their death. There is a sense in which our residents have reached a stage in their lives where they are living in the season of Advent a time of joyful hope, a time to open their hearts and welcome Jesus as their Saviour in preparation for meeting him soon. As chaplains and worship leaders serving in care homes we have the privilege of helping our residents to prepare themselves to meet Jesus and welcome him into their lives. This chapter offers worship resources for the four weeks of Advent and includes a Christingle Service. Resources for Christmas Carol Services and Nativity Services can be found in the Celebrating the Season of Christmas section although they will probably happen during Advent.

Planning Advent Services

Mood and atmosphere: A sense of anticipation and hope

Colours: Purple

Visual display: Advent wreath – light the candles for each week of Advent

Theme/ Story/ Message:
Jesus is the Light of the World
Repent and prepare for the coming of Jesus
Say "Yes" to Jesus

Bible Readings:
Isaiah 9: 2,6
John 3:16-17
Luke 3: 3-16
Luke 1: 26-38

Hymns:
Advent candles tell their story (Tune- Angel voices ever singing)
Lo, He comes with clouds descending
On Jordan's bank the Baptist's cry
Tell out my soul
Hills of the north rejoice

Songs:
May the Light of Christ shine in the darkness
The Lord is my light - Taize
The Christingle Song (Tune- Sing Hosanna)
Like a candle flame – Graham Kendrick
Jesus bids us shine
Colours of day
Shine Jesus shine
Give me oil in my lamp

Prayers:
Lighting of the 5 Advent Candles
[Some care homes don't allow real candles but LED candles can be used]
These candles represent love, joy, peace, hope and Jesus the light of the world.

Response: sung after each prayer

May the light of Christ shine in the darkness
May the light of Christ shine in our hearts

We light this first candle to remember God's love for us when he came into our world to be with us.....

We light this second candle to express our joy at his coming into our own lives......

We light this third candle to pray for peace in our world and in our own hearts.......

We light this fourth candle to pray for hope for all those who are suffering......

And we light the Christmas Day candle to welcome Jesus the light of the world into our lives.

Visual aids: Annunciation and Nativity pictures, the Christingle orange.

Activities and 3D ideas:
Making an Advent wreath
Making Christingles
Making Christmas cards

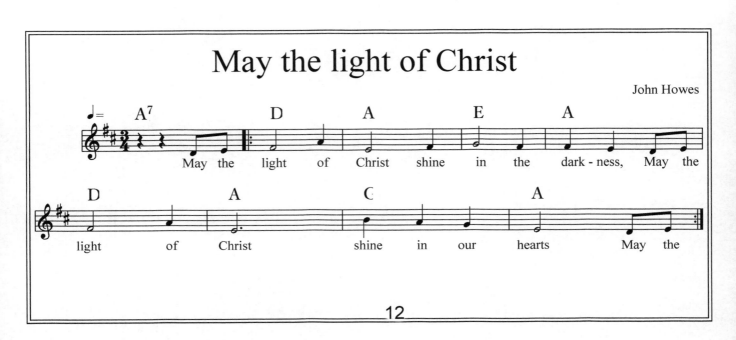

Advent Service
First week of Advent

Visual display - Advent wreath [Light one candle]

Welcome and Introduction

Light the First Candle of Advent:

All: **May the light of Christ shine in the darkness**
             May the light of Christ shine in our hearts

We light the first candle of Advent
To remember God's love for us when he came into our world to
be with us.

All: **May the light of Christ….**

Hymn: Advent Candles tell their story

Let us confess our sin:

Leader: Lord forgive us
All: **Lord forgive us and help us.**

For the times we have forgotten to love you and give you
thanks for all your goodness. Lord forgive us….

For the times we have been unkind or forgotten to love those
around us.
Lord forgive us…..

Lord forgive us and help us to love you and our neighbours
that we might grow together as a community of love and faith.

Reading: Isaiah 9: 2,6

Talk

Hymn: Shine Jesus shine

Prayers

Leader: Lord we pray to you

**All: May the light of Christ shine in the darkness
             May the light of Christ shine in our hearts**

Let us draw all these prayers together in the words of
The Lord's Prayer

All: Our Father who art in heaven….

Hymn: Lo he comes with clouds

Blessing
Leader: May the smile of God warm us
            May the light of Jesus lead us
            May the Holy Spirit blaze in our lives
            and fill us with love.
            Amen

All: The Grace

Talk

Well can you believe that it is already nearly December and the end of the year? This coming Sunday is Advent Sunday which marks the beginning of our preparations for the Christmas season.

Not many of you have the opportunity to go out to the shops now, but I can assure you that preparations for Christmas are in full swing in the big supermarkets. There are enormous Christmas trees and signs up telling us how many sleeps there are until Christmas, there is tinsel and baubles everywhere and at the local garden centre Santa is in his grotto being visited by excited children. Everyone suddenly becomes very busy at this time of year writing cards, buying presents and food.

But is this really what Advent is all about? The word advent means 'coming' and it is really about preparing for the coming of Jesus. But what does that actually mean for us here? What does it mean to prepare ourselves for the coming of Jesus? I have been pondering this question myself and I think that it is the complete opposite to what is happening in the shops: It's not about becoming very, very busy, but instead it is about slowing down and taking time to make our hearts ready to receive Jesus in a special way this Christmas. So, it's thinking about what Jesus means to us, thanking him for his presence in our lives. It's about putting ourselves right with God and with other people in our lives if we need to, doing a kind of spring clean of our hearts getting rid of any resentments or bitterness, asking God to help us to forgive if we need to. Also we have some special services coming up, a Christingle service next week, a carol service and a Nativity service where we will be telling the Christmas story and especially thanking Jesus for coming into our world and into our lives to be with us. These services are an opportunity to prepare ourselves to receive him and to worship him. In this place we are away from the hurly burly of the market place and so I would encourage you over the next few weeks to take some time to prepare yourselves to welcome Jesus into your hearts in a new way.

Our next song is all about Jesus the Light of the world coming into our lives.

Hymn: Shine Jesus shine

Prayers

Leader: Lord we pray to you

All: May the light of Christ shine in the darkness
**   May the light of Christ shine in our hearts**

As we come now to our time of prayer, let us thank Jesus for coming into our world, for coming as a baby, as one of us, for loving us and for being our Saviour.

Lord Jesus as we enter this Advent season we ask you to help us to prepare ourselves for your coming. May we open our hearts to receive you in a new way this Christmas. Lord we pray to you....

We think of our families, friends and loved ones at this busy time preparing to celebrate Christmas and ask that they would be especially blessed with your love, joy and peace. Lord we pray to you....

We pray for all those who care for us here, for staff and volunteers. Please bless them and their families. Lord we pray to you....

We pray for all those who are suffering at this time, for those in hospital, for those who are poor or homeless, for those who are lonely with no one to love them. Please be close to them we pray, and may they be helped and healed through the love of your people. Lord we pray to you ...

Let us draw all these prayers together in the words of the **Lord's Prayer.**

15

The Christingle

To find out more about the meaning of the Christingle, look at Christingle by Fr Simon Rundell on your You Tube browser. This video can be shown during a Christingle making activity or at the beginning of a Christingle service.

Christingle Service
Second week of Advent

Visual display: Advent wreath [Light 2 candles & Christingles]

Welcome and Introduction

Lighting the Advent Candles:

All: **May the light of Christ shine in the darkness**
May the light of Christ shine in our hearts

We light this first candle to remember God's love for us when he came into our world to be with us.

All: **May the light of Christ…..**

We light this second candle to express our joy at his coming.

All: **May the light of Christ…..**

We light all the Christingle candles to remind us that Jesus is the light of the world.

All: **May the light of Christ…..**

Hymn: Jesus bids us shine

Confession:
Leader: Lord forgive us….
All: **Lord forgive us and help us.**

Lord Jesus we come before you today just as we are with our strengths and weaknesses, our doubts and fears, our joys and sorrows.

For the times when we have closed ourselves to God and not loved him with all our heart.
Lord forgive us….

For the times when we have closed ourselves to one another and not loved one another fully.
Lord forgive us…

May God our Father forgive us and help us to love him and our neighbours here, that we might continue to grow together as a community of love and faith. **Amen**

Reading: John 3:16-17

Talk: The story of the Christingle

Song: The Christingle Song (Tune Sing Hosanna)

Prayers
Leader: Lord in your mercy
All: **Hear our prayer**

Let us draw all these prayers together in the words of
The Lord's Prayer

All: **Our Father who art in Heaven……**

Song: Colours of Day

Blessing:
                    May the smile of God warm us
                    May the light of Jesus lead us,
                    May the Holy Spirit blaze in our lives and fill us with love. **Amen**

All: **The Grace**

Talk

At the services I have been to in the past usually everyone in the congregation has a Christingle to hold. But we have to be a bit careful here. The manager wouldn't be too pleased if we set the building on fire, but as you can see we have put them all around the room. Doesn't the room look beautiful in the candlelight?

So, what is the meaning of the Christingle?
Can anyone tell me what the orange symbolises?
The orange symbolises our world, the world that God has made. The world where we live.

The red ribbon reminds us of the Easter story. It symbolises Jesus' suffering and death on the cross. And the red ribbon is wrapped around the orange which symbolises God's love which is wrapped all around the world. Like a circle, this love has no end it is eternal. Easter seems to be a long time ago now, but we had a beautiful celebration here on Good Friday, we gathered around the cross to think about Jesus and his death. So, the red ribbon reminds us of Easter.

Sticking into the orange are 4 sticks with fruits and sweets on. What do they represent?
The 4 sticks represent the 4 seasons of the year. Spring, summer, autumn, winter. And the fruits and sweets represent the food that God provides for us all year round. A couple of months ago we were celebrating Harvest and you may remember that we collected a big box of food which was donated by our friends and family and by the staff. We then gave this food to the food bank. We gave thanks for all God's provision for us and prayed for those in our world who don't have enough to eat. Each stick also has a jelly baby to represent the people on this earth, you and me. We are all God's children. He loves us and cares for us.

Finally, the candle. What does this represent?
It represents Jesus the light of the world coming into the world at Christmas. Our reading today tells us that God loved our world so much that he sent his son Jesus to come into our world. Jesus came to tell us about the love of God, he came to tell us that God is our Father and we are his children, he came to shine his light into all the dark places in our world and into all the dark times in our own lives. He came to bring us hope, to fill us with God's love.

Let's think about that as we sing the Christingle Song

Prayers

As we come now to our time of prayer, we give thanks for Jesus who came as a light into our world. May we open our hearts to receive his light and be filled with his love. Lord in your mercy.....

In this season of Advent, we especially think of our world and pray that as we draw near to Christmas that the light of Christ will burn ever brighter in our world to bring peace and goodwill to all people. Lord in your mercy......

We thank you that you made our world and encircled it with your everlasting love. Thank you that you are our Father and we are your children. Thank you for all your care and provision for our needs. Lord in your mercy.....

We pray for all those in our world who live in darkness. For those who are homeless, for those in prison, for those who are alone. We pray for those who suffer because of war, famine or natural disaster. Lord in your mercy....

We pray for the leaders of the nations that they may learn to work together for a more peaceful, fairer, more sustainable world. We pray that you will give them wisdom to find solutions to the present conflicts. Lord in your mercy......

Let us draw all these prayers together in the words of the **Lord's Prayer.**

John the Baptist
Third week of Advent

Visual display: Advent wreath - [Light three candles]

Welcome and Introduction

Lighting the Advent candles

All: **May the light of Christ shine in the darkness**
May the light of Christ shine in our hearts

We light the first candle of Advent to remember God's love for us when he came into our world to be with us.

All: **May the light of Christ….**

We light this second candle to express our joy at his coming into our own lives……

All: **May the light of Christ….**

We light this third candle to pray for peace in our world and in our own hearts…….

All: **May the light of Christ….**

Hymn: Advent candles tell their story (Tune: Angel voices)

Let us confess our sin:

Leader: Lord forgive us
All: **Lord forgive us and help us.**

For the times we have forgotten to love you and give you thanks for all your goodness.
Lord forgive us….   21

For the times we have been unkind or forgotten to love those around us.
Lord forgive us…..

Lord forgive us and help us to love you and our neighbours that we might grow together as a community of love and faith.

Reading: Luke 3: 3-16

Talk

Hymn: On Jordan's bank the Baptist's cry

Prayers
Leader: Lord in your mercy
All: Hear our prayer

Let us draw all these prayers together in the words of
The Lord's Prayer

All: Our Father who art in Heaven……

Hymn: Hills of the north rejoice

Blessing:
          May the smile of God warm us
          May the light of Jesus lead us,
          May the Holy Spirit blaze in our lives and fill us with love. **Amen**

All: The Grace

Talk

Luke 3: 3-16

Today we have the story of John the Baptist. He was a cousin of Jesus and was really the last of the Old Testament prophets. Before he was born his parents had been told by an angel that he would be a prophet and was especially called by God to prepare the people for the coming of their promised Messiah – the one they had all been waiting for.

As we have heard in this reading he was quite a fierce individual, a bit of a hell fire preacher, but what he was doing was to call people to repent, to turn away from sin, to clean up their lives and to come back to God with all their hearts, so that now they would be living for God rather than for themselves.

In this story, John the Baptist gives some practical advice on how to do this. He says if you have two tunics give one away to someone who has none. Share your food with people that have nothing to eat. He told the tax collectors to be honest and the soldiers to be content with their pay and not to take money from the people.

But I wonder what he would say to us? How would he advise us to prepare for the coming of Jesus?
We are living in a very different time and none of us are tax collectors or soldiers, but still we too are called to repent, to turn away from sin and to live our lives for God. I think if John the Baptist was here today he might say to us,
"Show care and consideration towards those you live with and if you have fallen out with someone then make up so you can live happily together.

If there is anyone in your family who you feel bitter towards or haven't spoken to for many years, then forgive and be reconciled.
If you haven't spoken to God or even thought about him for a long time, then take some time to pray and begin to get to know him again."

Advent is a time to prepare our hearts to meet Jesus, a time to get rid of anything in our lives that is stopping us from feeling close to him. If any of you would like some help to repent and turn again to Jesus, then do speak to one of us at the end of the service.

Prayers

As we come now to our time of prayer, we hear John the Baptist's call to us to repent and to turn back to God.

Heavenly Father, we thank you for this Advent season, a time to prepare our hearts to meet Jesus. We do indeed ask for your help to repent and to turn away from our sin and come back to you with all our hearts. Lord in your mercy....

Lord Jesus we welcome you into our hearts and pray that you would help us to live our lives with you and for you. Lord in your mercy......

We pray for all our families and friends who are busy at this time of year with all the preparations for Christmas. Please be close to them and remind them that you are the reason for the season. Lord in your mercy......

We pray for all those who care for us here, for managers, staff and volunteers. Please bless them with joy and peace. Lord in your mercy......

We draw all these prayers together in the words of the **Lord's Prayer.**

Mary
Fourth week of Advent

Visual display: Advent wreath – [light four candles]
Picture: The Annunciation - The Benedictine Nuns of Turvey Abbey.

Welcome and Introduction

Lighting the Advent candles:

All: May the light of Christ shine in the darkness
May the light of Christ shine in our hearts

We light the first candle of Advent to remember God's love for us when he came into our world to be with us.

All: May the light of Christ….

We light this second candle to express our joy at his coming into our own lives……

All: May the light of Christ….

We light this third candle to pray for peace in our world and in our own hearts…….

All: May the light of Christ….

We light this fourth candle to pray for hope for all those who are suffering……

All: May the light of Christ….

Hymn: Advent candles tell their story

Let us confess our sin:

Leader:	Lord forgive us
All:	**Lord forgive us and help us.**

For the times we have forgotten to love you and give you thanks for all your goodness….Lord forgive us….

For the times we have been unkind or forgotten to love those around us…Lord forgive us…..

Lord forgive us and help us to love you and our neighbours that we might grow together as a community of love and faith.

Reading:	Luke 1: 26- 38

Talk

Hymn:	Take my life and let it be

Prayers
Leader:	Lord in your mercy
All:	**Hear our prayer**

Let us draw all these prayers together in the words of
The Lord's Prayer

All:	**Our Father who art in Heaven……**

Hymn:	Tell out my soul

Blessing:

> May the smile of God warm us
> May the light of Jesus lead us,
> May the Holy Spirit blaze in our lives and fill us
> with love. **Amen**

All:	**The Grace**

Talk

Luke 1:26-38

This is the story of a young girl named Mary who lived in a small village called Nazareth in the north of Israel. Up to this point she was living a completely normal life. But then suddenly everything changes when she sees an angel - in fact the Angel Gabriel who had come as a special messenger from God. He tells her that God has especially noticed her and is pleased with her. He then goes on to say that she has been especially chosen by God to bring his own Son into the world.

Understandably she seems a bit confused at first. It's a lot to take in. What could it all possibly mean?
But the angel explains that the Holy Spirit will come upon her in a special way and then she will conceive and bear a son – God's own son who will become the Saviour of the world.

Can anyone remember what she says in response to this news?
She simply says 'Yes'.

I think that she must have known that it would not be easy to follow God's call. It must have been very hard to tell her parents and family knowing that they might not believe that she had seen an angel and might think the worst of her. We know that it was very hard for her to tell Joseph to whom she was engaged to be married. We know that at first, he didn't believe her story and wanted to divorce her. During her pregnancy it must have been very difficult to cope with the stares and slights of her friends and neighbours in Nazareth who probably would not have understood that God had called her to do this.
But in spite of all this she says 'Yes' to God because she believes what the angel has said to her.
She says, 'I am the Lord's servant, let it be to me as you have said.'
Mary has a special place in the Christmas story because she heard God calling her and she then gave her life to him. In fact, she brought Jesus into the world and then she brought him up to know and love God and to respond to his own calling to be our Saviour. She remained close to him during his mission and she was at the foot of the cross when he died. She kept saying 'Yes' to God right to the end.

Our next hymn – Take my life and let it be is an opportunity for each of us to say our own yes to Jesus and to give him our lives as Mary did.

Prayers

As we come to our time of prayer we thank God for Mary and ask that we might follow her example in giving our own lives to Jesus.

Heavenly Father, we thank you for this season of Advent, this time of preparing ourselves for the coming of Jesus at Christmas. Help us to say our own yes and to welcome Jesus into our lives. Lord on your mercy….

We pray for all those who are very busy preparing for Christmas perhaps feeling tired and stressed, may they and we find the time and space to prepare our hearts to receive Jesus. Lord in your mercy….

We pray for all those who have no home, no family, no friends, no church community and no reason to celebrate this Christmas. Please be very close to them and reach out to them with your love through your people. Lord in your mercy…..

CHRISTMAS

Celebrating the season of Christmas

Introduction

Christmas in care homes is often a time of mixed emotions for all those who live and work there. The staff do all they can to make the festive season bright and happy for the residents. Often residents will all be given a present and card, there will be special dinners and parties, choirs and children singing carols, entertainers and pantomimes. However, beneath all the joy and fun we can sometimes find a very real sadness. It is at Christmas time that residents can feel their loss of their loved ones more acutely. They may reminisce about family Christmases when they were growing up or when their own children were young. There can be a great sense of loss as they remember that their loved ones are no longer here, and they are now celebrating Christmas among strangers. Residents whose children or grandchildren live far away feel that distance and the sadness of knowing that their family will be gathering together without them.

As chaplains in care homes we are able to bring peoples' attention back to the stable in Bethlehem, to a family who were far from home. We tell the timeless story again of the Son of God, Jesus our Saviour coming to our world as a tiny baby, vulnerable, poor and weak. Jesus became human so that he could completely share in our life and our experiences as human beings. Especially he understands the frailty and vulnerability of the residents we are caring for. The message of Good News that we bring is that Jesus is Emmanuel – God with us, completely sharing in our lives. He too has experienced the weakness, sadness and loss that we go through especially in the last stages of life.

This chapter offers worship resources and reflections on the Nativity, Epiphany and infancy narratives which will take you through January into February.

Planning Christmas Services

Mood and atmosphere: Joy and celebration

Colours: Gold

Visual display:
> Pictures of the Nativity,
> Stable & nativity figures
> Wise men figures, presents
> Picture of the presentation of Jesus
> Picture of the baptism of the Lord
> Candles

Theme/ Story/ Message: Jesus our Saviour is born

Bible Readings:
The nativity narratives – Matt 1:18 – 2:12, Luke 2: 1- 2:52

Hymns: Christmas carols

Songs:

> Mary's boy child
> When a child is born
> Come and join the celebration
> Love Shone Down
> Mistletoe & Wine

Prayers:

> Prayers for peace in our world
> Prayers for those who are homeless or refugees
> Prayers for those who are lonely or far from home

Visual aids: A donkey! A baby.
> Percussion instruments, bells

Activities and 3D ideas:

> Making candle table arrangements
> Christmas crafts
> Making Christmas cards and presents
> Nativity plays and Christmas concerts
> with residents, staff and volunteers

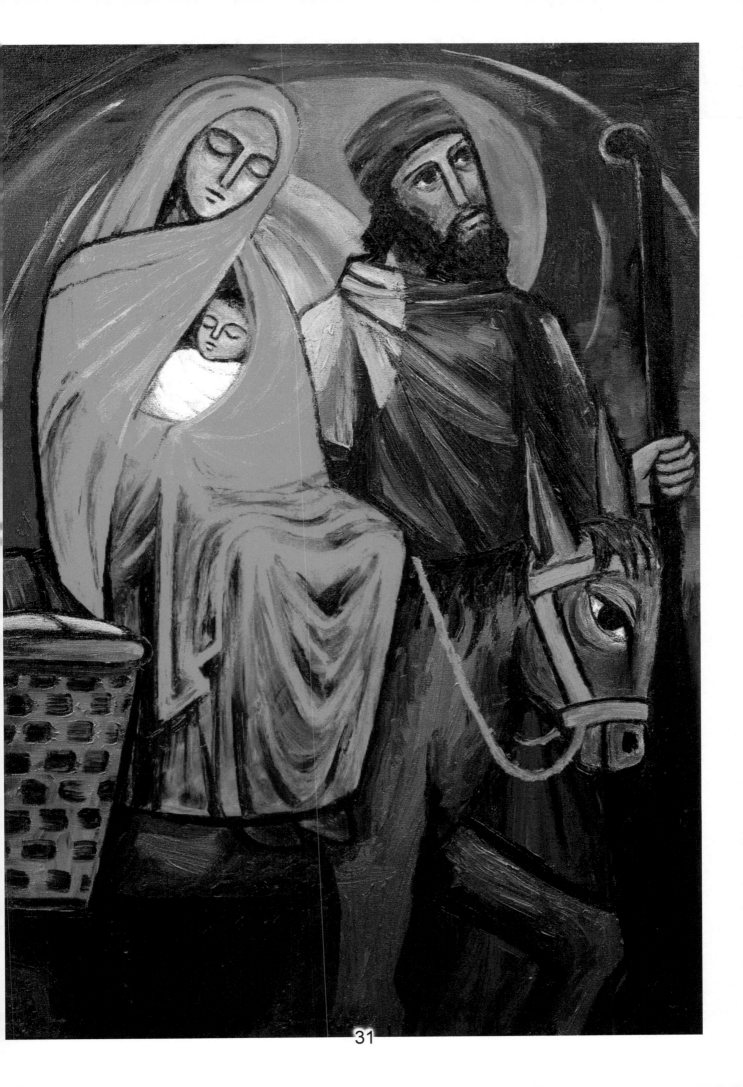

Carol Service

Welcome and Introduction

Carol: Once in Royal David's City

Reading: Luke 1: 26-38

Carol: The Angel Gabriel

Reading: Luke 2: 1-5

Carol: Little Donkey

Reading: Luke 2: 6-7

Carol: O Little Town of Bethlehem

Reading: Luke 2: 8-20

Carol: While shepherds watched

Reading: Matthew 2: 1-12

Carol: We three kings

Carol: Silent Night

Reading: Matthew 2: 13-15

Talk

Carol: O Come all ye faithful

Prayer and Blessing

The Grace

Carol Service Introduction and talk
(Recommended Third or Fourth Week of Advent)

Visual display: Advent wreath- [light 3 candles]

Picture: The flight to Egypt - The Benedictine Nuns of Turvey Abbey

Welcome and Introduction

Lighting the Advent Candles
These candles represent love, peace, joy and hope and the Christmas Day candle to welcome Jesus the light of the world

May the light of Christ shine in the darkness
May the light of Christ shine in our hearts

We light this first candle to remember God's love for us when he came into our world to be with us.
May the light of Christ….

We light this second candle to express our joy at his coming into our own lives.
May the light of Christ….

We light this third candle to pray for peace in our world and in our own hearts.
May the light of Christ….

Talk

Well it is so lovely to see so many of you here today for our carol service - residents and their relatives and friends and staff and volunteers.
Our service this afternoon has been an opportunity for some of us to come away from the busyness of our preparations for Christmas and for all of us to listen again to the timeless story of Jesus' birth as told in the readings and the carols. It is the simple but extraordinary story of God coming to our world as one of us, making himself little and vulnerable and needing to be cared for, just like us, having to rely on others, to put his life into the hands of others and to trust them just as we do here. It is for this reason that Jesus is able to share in our life here, he is close to us. He lives here with us and he knows all about our difficulties and struggles and he loves us.

It was a great joy and privilege for Mary and Joseph to care for Jesus and to bring him up. In a similar way it is a joy and privilege for us as staff and volunteers to care for all of you residents. And I wanted to say a very big thank you to our wonderful staff for all the tender loving care which they give to us and for all the ways in which they constantly go the extra mile to make us happy and comfortable. And I wanted to say a big thank you to our volunteers who give up so much of their time to be with us and to enrich our lives with the activities, music and services.

But also, I am so aware of residents expressing care for one another and concern for staff around them and I am aware of friendships being formed between us. And all of this is building up our community life together.

Jesus came into our world with a simple message of good news for everyone. That good news is God loves us, and he is always with us. It is this love and his presence with us that enables us all to go on loving and caring for one another here. And it is this love which makes this home such a special place to be.

So, as we approach Christmas let us give thanks for Jesus, that he came into our world, that he is here among us now, and that we are loved by God and by one another and that we belong to this community.

May I finish by wishing you and your families all a very Joyful Christmas and a happy, healthy and peaceful year to come.

Our final carol is: O Come all ye faithful.

Blessing

> May the joy of the angels,
> The wonder of the shepherds
> And the peace of the Christ Child
> Fill our hearts this Christmas time
> And may God's blessing be with us and all those we love
> Now and for always
> Amen

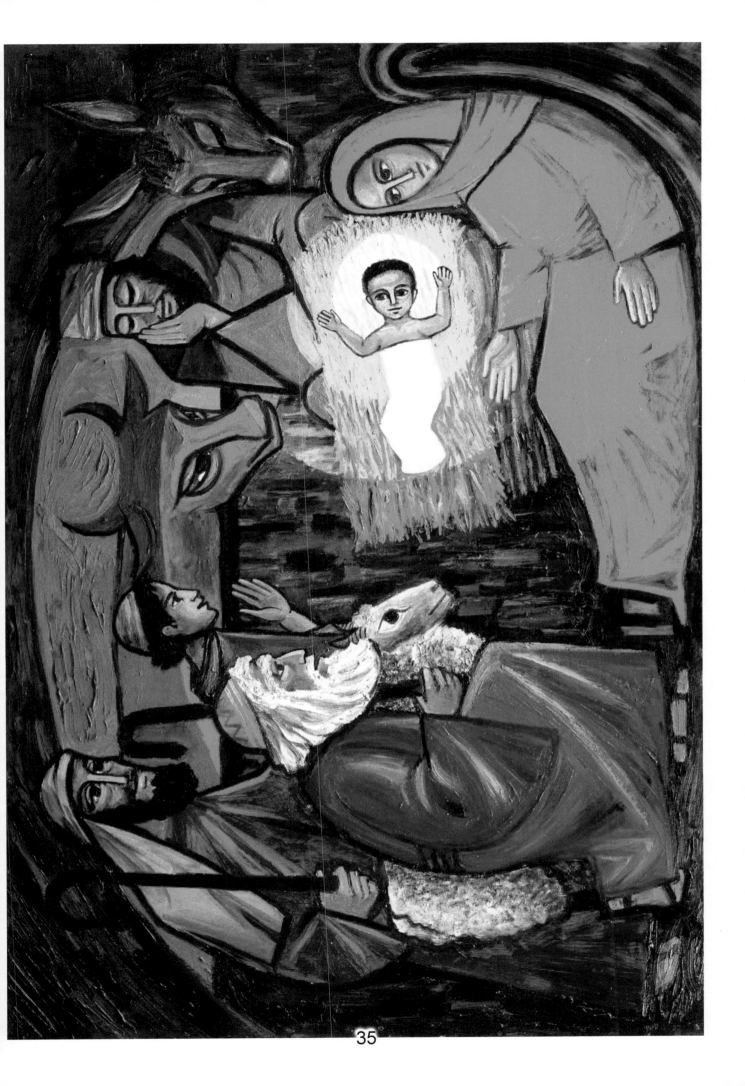

Nativity Service
Christmas Week

Visual Display: Advent wreath with 5 candles lit, Nativity set

Picture: The Nativity - The Benedictine Nuns of Turvey Abbey

Welcome and Introduction

Song: Come and join the celebration

Prayer:
Loving Father, as we prepare, once again, to celebrate the birth of your son in Bethlehem, make us ready to receive him in our hearts and in this home, that he may dwell with us forever. As we hear that familiar story once again, may we be inspired by your gift of love and be ready to respond with lives of joyful service to one another. **Amen.**

Lighting of the 5 Advent Candles
These candles represent love, joy, peace, hope and Jesus the light of the world…..

All: **May the light of Christ shine in the darkness,
          May the light of Christ shine in our hearts**

We light this first candle to remember God's love for us when he came into our world to be with us…..

We light this second candle to express our joy at his coming into our own lives……

We light this third candle to pray for peace in our world and in our own hearts…….

We light this fourth candle to pray for hope for all those who are suffering……

And we light the Christmas Day candle to welcome Jesus the light of the world into our lives.

Reading: Luke 2: 1-7

Carol: Away in a Manger

Talk

Carol: The first Nowell

Prayers:

All: O Come let us adore him   x3
**   Christ the Lord**

The Lord's Prayer

Carol: Hark the Herald

Blessing:

             May the joy of the angels,
             the wonder of the shepherds,
             and the peace of the Christ Child,
             fill your hearts this Christmas time;
             and may God's blessing be with you,
             now and for always.
             Amen

All: The Grace

Talk

You may remember right at the beginning of December we talked about Advent being a time to prepare ourselves for the coming of Jesus into our lives at Christmas and it has been a lovely time. A couple of weeks ago we had our Christingle service. We lit lots of candles and remembered that Jesus is the light of the world and we prayed that Jesus' light would come into all the dark places of our world. Last week we had our lovely carol service where we told the Christmas story with readings from the Bible and sang lots of carols. Today we think about what really happened. We know that Mary was pregnant and that together she and Joseph had to make a very long journey - about 100 hundred miles to Bethlehem and when they got there, there was nowhere for them to stay. They must have felt desperate. In the end all there was was a stable which would have been like a cave at the back of the inn- a place for the animals.
It is a story we are all so familiar with, that we acted out as children in nativity plays and that we have read and sung about all our lives.

But have you ever wondered what it all really meant? Well, it is the story of what happened when God decided to make himself human. He came into our world as a baby just like we all did. Its an extraordinary thing isn't it – what was God thinking of? He made himself very small, very weak and vulnerable, to become one of us, so that he could totally share in our lives here in this world. So that he could be with us all the time, in everything we ourselves go through in our lives. He did this because he no longer wanted to be a God who was distant, somehow separate from us, someone we couldn't really relate to, but he wanted to be close to us, to love us, to share our lives with us. So, he came in the person of Jesus. Perhaps there have been times in your life when you have felt that God has been close to you. Sometimes I have been aware that God is close to us here when we worship him together. Maybe some of you have felt that too.

When Jesus came as a baby, he was not born into a wealthy or important family and the only people who knew about it at the time were a bunch of rather ragged shepherds who came down from the hillsides and some foreign gentlemen, astronomers from Persia which is modern day Iraq. What God was thinking and why he chose them to be at his birth. I don't know. But there was an openness in them to what God was doing. They heard the good news that the Saviour of the world had been born, they believed, and they came to see him. And when they saw him, they worshipped him.

So today, just like the shepherds and wise men we ourselves have come to the stable. We have seen the Saviour. We have believed in him and now we worship him

Carol: The First Nowell

Prayers

Leader: Jesus we adore you

All: sing   **O come let us adore him x3**
                    Christ the Lord

Lord Jesus as we gather to worship you this Christmas we thank you for coming to our world as a baby, for becoming one of us and for sharing in our lives. Jesus, we adore you….

We thank you that you are always with us, that you know us each one by name, that you are close to us and you love us. Please fill our hearts with joy this Christmas. Jesus, we adore you……

Jesus when you came you were homeless and very poor. We pray for all those today who are homeless and poor, for refugees who are far from home, for those who are lonely and have no one to love them. Be close to them we pray. Jesus, we adore you…..

The Lord's Prayer.

Epiphany Service

Picture: The Magi - The Benedictine Nuns of Turvey Abbey

Welcome and Introduction

Opening responses

Leader: With the wise men who came from afar
            We are seeking Jesus
All: We are seeking Jesus

Leader: At the beginning of a new day
            We are seeking Jesus
All: We are seeking Jesus

Leader: At the beginning of a new year
            We are seeking Jesus
All: We are seeking Jesus

Carol: The first Nowell

Confession.
Leader: Lord forgive us
All: Lord forgive us and help us.

Lord Jesus we come before you today just as we are with our strengths and weaknesses, our doubts and fears, our joys and sorrows.

For the times when we have closed ourselves to God and not loved him with all our heart. Lord forgive us....

For the times when we have closed ourselves to one another and not loved one another fully. Lord forgive us...

May God our Father forgive us and help us to love him and our neighbours here, that we might continue to grow together as a community of love and faith. **Amen**

Reading: Matthew 2: 1-12

Talk

Carol: As with gladness

Prayers:
Response: Lord in your mercy
All: **Hear our prayer**

The Lord's Prayer

Carol: We three kings

Blessing:
Lord God of heaven and earth, you revealed your only Son to every nation by the guidance of a star. Bless this home and all who live and work here. Fill us with the light of Christ, that our concern for one another may reflect your love.

May Christ Jesus dwell with us, keep us from harm, and make us one in mind and heart, now and forever.
Amen.

All: The Grace

Talk

Some of you may have noticed as you came into the lounge today that I have put some signs above the doors and there is one here on the wall. It says, 'Christ Bless This House.'

When I was preparing for this service today, I discovered that it is a custom in some churches to bless chalk and then to write above the doorways of people's homes either the initials of the 3 wise men traditionally known as Caspar, Melchior and Baltazar or to write these words Christ bless this house.

When I discovered this, I thought how appropriate it would be for us to begin the new year by praying for a blessing over our home here and over all of us who live and work here. So, in a moment during our prayers we will bless our home and one another and pray that we may be a blessing to all those who come to visit us here.

But before we do that we will sing on the sheets, 'As with gladness men of old' which is a carol telling of the wise men who came from the East, who brought precious gifts of gold, frankincense and myrrh and who came to worship and adore the Christ child. This carol is inviting us to do the same thing; to come to Jesus as we are, to offer ourselves to him and to worship him. So, let's do that as we sing together.

Carol: As with gladness

Prayers

Leader: Lord in your mercy,
All: Hear our prayer.

At the beginning of this New Year we dedicate our home, all of us who live and work here, and all our relatives, friends and loved ones who visit us here, to Christ Jesus our Lord. We pray that Jesus may be at the very heart of our home. Lord in your mercy....

We pray that this home may be filled with the love of Christ and that all may feel they belong as we work to build a community of love and faith. May we be at peace with one another as we live and work together. Lord in your mercy...

We pray that all who come to our home this year may experience Christ's welcome, his love, joy and peace. Lord in your mercy....

Lord Jesus we pray that you would bless us with good health and strength, surround us with your goodness, protect us from all harm and keep us close to you all the days of our life.
Amen

The Lord's Prayer

Simeon & Anna
The Presentation of the Lord

"Sovereign Lord, as you have promised, you may now dismiss your servant in peace. For my eyes have seen your salvation, which you have prepared in the sight of all nations: a light for revelation to the Gentiles and the glory of your people Israel." Luke 2: 29-32

Picture: The Presentation of the Lord -   The Benedictine Nuns
                                                                of Turvey Abbey

Welcome and Introduction

Opening Responses:

Leader: In our watching
                In our waiting
All: **God is alive in us**

Leader: In our questioning
                In our hoping
All: **God is alive in us**

Leader: In our travelling
                In our homecoming
All: **God is alive in us**

Hymn: Be still for the presence of the Lord

Confession:
Leader: Lord forgive us
All: **Lord forgive us and help us.**

Lord Jesus we come before you today just as we are with our strengths and weaknesses, our doubts and fears, our joys and sorrows.

For the times when we have closed ourselves to God and not loved him with all our heart. Lord forgive us....

For the times when we have closed ourselves to one another and not loved one another fully. Lord forgive us…

May God our Father forgive us and help us to love him and our neighbours that we might continue to grow together as a community of love and faith.
Amen

Reading: Luke 2: 22-39

Talk

Hymn: Taize

**Wait for the Lord
Whose day is near
Wait for the Lord
Keep watch, take heart**

Prayers
Leader: Lord we pray to you
All: **Wait for the Lord……**

Let us draw all these prayers together in the words of
The Lord's Prayer.

All: **Our Father who art in Heaven……**

Hymn: Shine Jesus shine

Blessing: May the Lord bless us and keep us
May the Lord make his face to shine upon us
and be gracious to us
May the Lord lift up the light of his countenance on
us and give us peace.

All: **The Grace**

Talk

The story of the presentation of the Lord in the temple, really completes the Christmas story. If you notice, the focus of the story is not so much on Jesus, but on two very old people - Simeon and Anna. In fact these people were the same sort of age as all of you are. Like you they had lived a long life and like you they were very wise. So I wonder if they have anything to teach us or to show us.

I notice that they both spent their retirement and old age in the temple. Every day they were there worshipping and praying. The very active time of their lives were over. They had retired from work. They had raised their children. They had been active in their community and now all that activity was over. Many of us who are living very busy, active lives do not have the time to do what they were doing, to spend time praying and worshipping God. I do believe that Simeon and Anna are an example to us of old age lived very well. This slower time is spent praying and being with the Lord. This stage of life can be such a blessing and a time of being close to God

What else were they doing? They were waiting. What were they waiting for? They were waiting for Jesus. Simeon knew that he wouldn't die until he had seen the coming of the Messiah and so there he was waiting every day for the day when he would see Jesus. He was actively waiting with his eyes open. The wonderful thing is that when Mary and Joseph and the baby Jesus came into the temple that day both he and Anna recognised him. They knew who he was. They were ready to meet him. Again I believe that Simeon and Anna are an example to us of very old people who were ready and waiting for Jesus. They lived in a state of hope and anticipation They encourage all of us whether we are young or old to be ready to meet Jesus, to be actively waiting and to wait in a spirit of hope not despair. It is never too late to welcome Jesus into our hearts. When we invite him with a simple prayer **Lord Jesus come into my heart**, he will help us to live this time of old age with all the difficulties and challenges it brings with great hope and joy.

Prayers Taize:

Wait for the Lord
His day is near
Wait for the Lord
Keep watch
Take heart

As we come now to our time of prayer we thank God for the inspiration that Simeon and Anna are for us, for the life they lived well in their very old age and for the hope they held in their hearts of one day seeing the promised Messiah. We pray that we may hold this hope in our own hearts as we pray with them Thy kingdom come. Lord we pray to you.....**Wait for the Lord**.....

Lord Jesus as we come to the end of this Christmas time, we thank you that you did come 2000 years ago. We pray that you would come in a special way into our own hearts as we pray, **Lord Jesus come into my heart.** Lord we pray to you......**Wait for the Lord**.....

We pray for all the residents, living in this care home. We pray that in this time of waiting you will all come to know how much God loves you. We pray that your lives would be filled with meaning and hope. Lord we pray to you.......**Wait for the Lord**.....

We pray for all the volunteers as we serve the Lord here, that we would be bearers of Christ's light and hope to all those who feel sad and alone. Lord we pray to you.....**Wait for the Lord**....

The Boy Jesus
Found in the Temple

Welcome and Introduction

Opening Responses:

Leader: Young and old
                  Friends and strangers
All: **God welcomes us**

Leader: Lost and bewildered
                  Found and rejoicing
All: **God welcomes us**

Leader: This morning, this day
                  This night, forever
All: **God welcomes us**

Hymn: Great is thy faithfulness

Confession:

Leader: Lord forgive us
All: **Lord forgive us and help us.**

Lord Jesus we come before you today just as we are with our strengths and weaknesses, our doubts and fears, our joys and sorrows.

For the times when we have closed ourselves to God and not loved him with all our heart. Lord forgive us….

For the times when we have closed ourselves to one another and not loved one another fully. Lord forgive us…

May God our Father forgive us and help us to love him and our neighbours that we might continue to grow together as a community of love and faith. **Amen**

Reading: Luke 2: 41-52

Talk

Hymn: Jesus good above all other

Prayers:
Leader: Lord in your mercy
All: **Hear our prayer**

Let us draw all these prayers together in the words of
The Lord's Prayer

All: **Our Father who art in Heaven……**

Hymn: Lord of all hopefulness

Blessing: May the Lord bless us and keep us
May the Lord make his face to shine upon us
and be gracious to us
May the Lord lift up the light of his countenance
on us and give us peace. **Amen**

All: **The Grace**

Talk

This is the last of the Bible readings about Jesus' childhood. In this story Jesus is about 12 years old and he and his parents have travelled with a big crowd of friends and neighbours from Nazareth to Jerusalem – about 100 miles. It would have taken a few days to make the journey on foot. They had come for the special celebration of Passover and so Jerusalem would have been heaving with people. When the festival is all over, the group from Nazareth begin the journey back and Mary and Joseph go with them assuming that Jesus is somewhere there in the crowd. But after while they realise that he isn't there. We can imagine them asking everyone if they have seen Jesus and people saying, "Well no, come to think of it I haven't seen him for a while." So, Mary and Joseph turn back to Jerusalem and begin searching for him there. The Bible says they looked for three days. I imagine they must have been absolutely frantic!

Probably some of you can remember losing a child, either your own or another child in your care and you can perhaps identify with the anxiety and feelings of panic that Mary and Joseph must have felt......
Tell stories of losing children.....

Mary and Joseph must have been so surprised to find Jesus in the Temple talking to the religious leaders clearly with no thought of them. They are even more surprised by his response when they ask him where he has been.

"Didn't you know, haven't you guessed that I would be here – in my Father's house?"

The Bible says that Mary treasured all these things in her heart- which means she mulled it over, kept remembering and thinking about what these extraordinary things might mean. I think for Mary; this incident must have been a little lesson in letting go. She knew that she had been asked to bring God's own son into the world and to bring him up and some extraordinary things had happened to her which she was treasuring in her heart, but she had to learn that she could not hold onto him, he had come for all mankind and that he would grow up and leave her to fulfil his mission. This is perhaps something that those of us who are parents have had to learn too. We have had to learn to let our own children go so that they too can grow up and leave us. But I do believe that all of us here still have an important role to play in praying for our loved ones - our children, grandchildren, nieces and nephews and so on. We can pray for them to come to know God as their Father, to become all that God wants them to be and do the things in life that he wants them to do.

Prayers:

As we come to our time of prayer, we think of Jesus who like us grew up in an ordinary family and who as he grew came to know God as his Father....

Heavenly Father we thank you for our own families, for our parents, our brothers and sisters and for all those who have loved, supported and guided us throughout our lives. Lord in your mercy....

We pray for our own children and grandchildren and all those who we have helped influence and guide. Please bless them, protect them and keep them close to you all the days of their lives. Lord in your mercy....

We pray for all those who care for us here, for staff and volunteers. Please fill them with your love, patience and compassion and bless them and their families. Lord in your mercy....

We pray for all those who are suffering, especially we think of those in hospital or prison, those who are homeless or who have no one to love them. May they know your comfort, hope and peace. Lord in your mercy....

The Lord's Prayer

The Baptism of the Lord
Beloved Children of God

Picture: The Baptism of the Lord -   The Benedictine Nuns of
                                                              Turvey Abbey

*And a voice from heaven said, "This is my beloved Son: with him I am well
pleased." Matt 3:17*

Welcome and Introduction

Opening Responses:

Leader:	The Lord is here among us
All:	**He calls us by name**

Leader:	The Lord loves us
All:	**He calls us by name**

Leader:	The Lord is always with us
All:	**He calls us by name**

Hymn:	Great is thy faithfulness

Confession:

Leader:	Lord forgive us
All:	**Lord forgive us and help us.**

Lord Jesus we come before you today just as we are with our
strengths and weaknesses, our doubts and fears, our joys and
sorrows.

For the times when we have closed ourselves to God and not
loved him with all of our heart. Lord forgive us….

For the times when we have closed ourselves to one another
and not loved one another fully. Lord forgive us…

May God our Father forgive us and help us to love him and our neighbours that we might continue to grow together as a community of love and faith. **Amen**

Reading: Matt 3:13-17

Talk

Hymn: **Father we adore you**
Lay our lives before you
How we love you.

Jesus we adore……

Spirit we adore…..

Prayers
Leader: Lord in your mercy
All: **Hear our prayer**

Let us draw all these prayers together in the words of
The Lord's Prayer

All: **Our Father who art in Heaven……**

Hymn: He's got the whole world

A blessing from Isaiah 43: God says to us…..

            Fear not for I have redeemed you
            I have called you by name
            You are mine.
            You are precious and honoured in my sight
            and I love you. May God bless us and keep us
            and hold us in the palm of his hand.

All: **The Grace**

Talk

Look at the picture of Jesus' baptism.
John the Baptist
The River Jordan

The people of Israel were brought up in the Jewish faith. They believed in God, but baptism was a sign that people wanted to turn back to God and make a new start. To get rid of their sins. Water was a sign that they could be washed clean.

Often people are baptised when they are babies, but some are baptised as adults. Can any of you remember your baptism?......

Jesus did not need to repent and turn back to God. So what did baptism mean for him? He was offering himself to God saying, "Here I am Father, please do your work through me, please glorify your name in me. Please lead people to you because of me." As he offered himself to God, something wonderful happened....
A dove rested on him and they heard the voice of the Father saying, "This is my beloved son in whom I am well pleased."

The good news is that it is never too late to repent and turn back to God. We are never too old to offer ourselves to God and to say, "Here I am Father. Please do your work in me. Please glorify your name through me. Please lead people to you because of me."

The other good news is that we are God's children – his sons and daughters. He says to us, "You are my beloved sons, my beloved daughters and I am very pleased with you.

Prayers

Leader: Lord in your mercy,
All: Hear our prayer.

As we come to this time of prayer, we thank God that he is our Father and we are his beloved sons and daughters.

Heavenly Father, we thank you that you know each one of us by name and that you love us so much. May each of us come to know that you are our Father and that we are your precious children. Lord in your mercy.....

We thank you for our home here. We pray that we would feel comfortable, contented and at peace as we live here together Lord in your mercy.....

We pray for all those who care for us – the managers, staff and volunteers. Please bless them in their work and fill them with your tender love and compassion. Lord in your mercy.....

We pray for all our families, friends and loved ones that you would be close to them and give them your strength and support. Lord in your mercy...

The Lord's Prayer

LENT

Celebrating the Season of Lent
Introduction

Lent in care homes begins on Shrove Tuesday with the tradition of making and eating pancakes, but after this, there is little or no understanding of what the season of Lent means.

Traditionally Lent is a time of preparation for Easter which entails prayer, fasting and alms giving. In our personal lives some of us will think of giving up something or perhaps taking on something new or establishing a good habit. We may eat simply one day per week and give some money to a charity. In our churches some of us may join an extra prayer or Bible study group. We may seek to simplify our lives in order to make some space for God.

But what does the season of Lent mean for those living in residential care and whose lives are structured and regimented by the routines of the home? In many ways the lives of our residents have already become very simple, the busy activity of daily life has come to an end. Work has finished and children and grandchildren are grown up. Much of life has already been stripped away. People have slowed down and now have space and time for reflection. The season of Lent encourages them and us in this reflection and so as chaplains we can slow down with our residents and with them take time to pray. We may suggest ways of doing this alone or together.

We also encourage our residents to prepare themselves for Easter by coming and sharing in worship. In our services we explore the Lenten themes of repentance, forgiveness and coming home to the father. Some residents have had the experience of receiving ashes on their forehead, but many have not, so often on Ash Wednesday we just make a sign of the cross on their foreheads and speak the words - "You belong to God."

When we come to Holy Week, we try to relive that last week of Jesus' life with its mixed emotions - the exuberance and joy of Palm Sunday, the intimacy of the Last Supper with the sharing of communion and the washing of the feet, the solemnity of Good Friday as we gather together around the cross and the joy of the resurrection on Easter Sunday.

Planning Lenten Services

Mood and atmosphere: Reflective

Colours: Purple

Visual displays: Pictures depicting gospel stories

Theme/ Story/ Message:

Homecomings
Lost and found
Repentance and forgiveness
Preparing for Easter

Other celebrations:

Mothering Sunday
St. Patrick's Day

Hymns:

Amazing grace, Just as I am,
I heard the voice of Jesus say,
The King of love,
The Lord's my shepherd,
Be thou my vision, I cannot tell,
Christ be beside me,
O love that wilt not let me go,
He's got the whole world.

Other music:

'

I'm coming home to my father'
by Mike Stanley CJM.
Irish music

Visual aids

A sign of the cross on people's
foreheads on Ash Wednesday

Activities and 3D ideas:

Mothering Sunday - Flower arranging groups,
flowers distributed by children
or members of local churches.
Posies of flowers made by more able
residents for other residents in the home.
Dramatic reading and story telling

Ash Wednesday Service

Pictures: Return of the Prodigal Son by Rembrandt
The Prodigal Son by The Benedictine Nuns of
Turvey Abbey

Welcome and Introduction

Opening Responses:

Leader: From dust we came,
To dust we will return
All: We belong to God

Leader: We gather in penitence,
We gather in confidence
All: We belong to God

Leader: At the beginning of Lent,
At every moment of our lives
All: We belong to God

Hymn: Great is thy faithfulness

Confession:

Leader: Lord forgive us
All: Lord forgive us and help us.

Lord Jesus we come before you today just as we are with our strengths and weaknesses, our doubts and fears, our joys and sorrows.

For the times when we have closed ourselves to God and not loved him with all of our heart. Lord forgive us….

For the times when we have closed ourselves to one another and not loved one another fully. Lord forgive us…

May God our Father forgive us and help us to love him and our neighbours that we might grow together as a community of love and faith. **Amen**

61

Reading: Luke 15: 11-32 – The Prodigal Son
                (told as a story)

Talk:

Hymn: Just as I am

During the hymn the chaplain will bless each person with the sign of the cross on their forehead and the words; "You belong to God"

Prayers:

Leader: Lord in your mercy
All: **Hear our prayer**

Let us draw all these prayers together in the words of The Lord's Prayer

All: **Our Father who art in Heaven…**

Hymn: Amazing grace

Closing Responses:

Leader: Marked by a cross
                Cherished and forgiven
All: **We are coming home**

Leader: Called to be holy,
                Called to be happy
All: **We are coming home**

Leader: God in our hearts,
                God in our lives
All: **We are coming home**

Blessing:
May the Father bless us, for he has adopted us as his children. May the Son come to help us, for he has received us as brothers and sisters. May the Spirit be with us, for he has made us his dwelling place.

All: **The Grace**

Introduction to the service

Today is a special service for Ash Wednesday which traditionally marks the beginning of Lent. Did you all enjoy some pancakes on Shrove Tuesday?

Lent begins 6 weeks before Easter and is an opportunity to take some time to prepare ourselves to celebrate the death and resurrection of Jesus which is the very heart of our faith.

Our theme today is 'We belong to God.' He is our Father and we are his children, so we begin with the response 'We belong to God.'

Talk- Telling the story of the Prodigal Son

As you were arriving today, I came around to show you my picture of the Prodigal Son coming home to the father.

I am not actually going to read the story from the Bible because it is very long. But it is a story of a man who owned a large farm and a lot of land. He has two sons who work with him on the farm. The older boy, not in this picture is a very dutiful son who works hard, is very responsible and who stays at home to look after his father in his old age. The younger boy is the complete opposite. He is restless and longs to get away and travel the world. He longs for fun and excitement. One day he tells his father that he is leaving and asks if he can have his inheritance now rather than waiting until his father dies. So with a very heavy heart the Father divides the property in two and gives the younger son his half. We know the story, the younger one goes off without so much as a backward glance, travels the world and spends all the money on a wild lifestyle. He has plenty of friends until the day comes when the money is all gone. His friends all disappear at this point and leave him with absolutely nothing. The boy becomes very hungry and homeless. In the end he is so desperate that he hires himself as a labourer on a pig farm. It is an awful life and he is still hungry. He begins to think of home. He starts to really miss his father. In the end he comes to his senses and decides to go home. On the way he is rehearsing what he will say when he gets home. He is going to say, "Father I have sinned against Heaven and against you. I am no longer worthy to be called your son, but let me be one of your servants."

Meanwhile back at the farm, the father was heart broken when his son left home. He worries about his son and longs for him to come home. Everyday he goes to the end of the road and looks and looks to see if his son is coming home. Until one day there he is in the distance. The father can hardly believe it. He forgets his age and literally runs to meet his son.

This picture shows us their meeting. The son tries to make his little speech about not being worthy to be called his son. But the father ignores this. He wraps his arms around his son and kisses him. When I showed you the picture earlier we particularly noticed that the son is very ragged, no shoes, he is dirty and covered with sores, he is sobbing on his father's shoulder. But here is the father holding him and saying "Its alright, it's alright. You're home, you're safe now. I forgive you.

When Jesus told this story it was to tell us about what God our Father is like, so full of love and compassion. None of us have ever seen God's face, but the artist has managed to show us what God's face looks like.

I often think that the lives we live on this earth are a bit like the journey home made by this boy. Things sometimes happen to us in life that leave us a bit ragged. Some of us have had some knocks that have left us a bit bruised and broken like this boy. There are times when we may have felt deserted and alone. But the good news is that when each of us finally make it home, this is what will happen. We will be caught up and held in the arms of the father and his face will look so compassionately at us because he will know all that we have been through on the journey home.
God loves us so much.

We now sing together the hymn Just as I am.

Prayers

Heavenly Father as we begin this season of Lent, we thank you that you are our Father and we are your children, we belong to you. Thank you that you open your arms wide to welcome us home.

Leader: Lord in your mercy
All: Hear our prayer

We thank you that you loved the world so much that you sent your son Jesus to come and be with us. Please be close to us and help us as we prepare ourselves for Easter, and as we remember his death and resurrection.

Leader: Lord in your mercy
All: Hear our prayer

We pray for all those who care for us here. Thank you for their dedication and loving care. Please bless them and their families. Please give them your gentleness, patience and compassion and help them to be happy in their work.

Leader: Lord in your mercy
All: Hear our prayer

We pray for our families, friends and all our loved ones. Please keep them all in your loving care.

Leader: Lord in your mercy
All: Hear our prayer

We pray for all those known to us who are suffering in anyway in body, mind or spirit. Please touch them with your peace, your strength and healing. May they be aware of your presence near to them.

Leader: Lord in your mercy
All: Hear our prayer

We pray for all those in need, especially for all those in our world today who are far from home. We pray for those who feel lonely, unloved and who have no one to pray for them. We pray for all the churches and other charities who are working to alleviate their suffering. We pray for justice and peace and an end to poverty in our world.

Leader: Lord in your mercy
All: Hear our prayer

We draw all these prayers together in the words of **The Lord's Prayer.**

The Parable of the Loving Father

Pictures: The Return of the Prodigal Son by Rembrandt
             The Prodigal Son by The Benedictine Nuns of
                                                Turvey Abbey

Welcome and Introduction

Opening Responses:

Leader: We come as ourselves
             We come as we are
All: **God welcomes us home**

Leader: Wherever we have been
             Whatever we have done
All: **God welcomes us home**

Leader: Lost and afraid
             Found and rejoicing
All: **God welcomes us home**

Hymn: Amazing Grace

Confession:

Leader: Lord forgive us

All: **Lord forgive us and help us.**

Lord Jesus we come before you today just as we are with our strengths and weaknesses, our doubts and fears, our joys and sorrows.

For the times when we have closed ourselves to God and not loved him with all of our heart. Lord forgive us….

For the times when we have closed ourselves to one another and not loved one another fully. Lord forgive us…

May God our Father forgive us and help us to love him and our neighbours that we might grow together as a community of love and faith. **Amen**

Reading: Luke 15: 11 - 32

Talk

Hymn: I Heard the voice of Jesus

Prayers:

Leader: Lord in your mercy
All: **Hear our prayer**

Let us draw these prayers together in the words of
The Lord's Prayer

Hymn: Just as I am

Blessing:

May the Father bless us, for he has adopted us
as his children. May the Son come to help us,
for he has received us as brothers and sisters.
May the Spirit be with us, for he has made us
his dwelling place.

All: **The Grace**

Talk

Luke 15: 11 - 32

This story is the very well known Parable of the Prodigal Son.
We know the story well. The younger son takes his share of his inheritance and breaks his Father's heart by leaving home and squandering all the money on wild living. While the older dutiful boy stays at home to work on the farm and look after his Father.

Probably all of us here can identify with one or more of the characters in the story. But today I would like us to focus on the Father. Everyday the Father went down to the bottom of the road to see if his son was coming home. When at last he sees his son in the distance he runs to meet him. Here in this picture we can see the son all ragged and poor and starving. The Father wraps him up in a huge hug. As I bring around the picture notice the absolute tenderness and compassion in the face of the Father.

But also he has the same expression for the older brother too who was full of anger and bitterness and was refusing to come home. To him he says "My son you have always been with me and everything I have is yours." The older brother was welcomed home too.

I don't know about you, but sometimes when life is difficult I feel a bit like this son, a bit ragged, afraid, alone. This image of God really helps me. Sometimes in my prayer times I come to the Father like this and say sorry for all that's wrong and talk to him about my feelings and struggles and I like to imagine myself swept up into the embrace of the Father. In this picture I think he is whispering into the son's ear, "It's alright. I know all about it. I know what you are going through. It's alright you're home now, all is well now." He speaks to us in the same way. He wants all of us to come home, to be close to him, to know how much he loves us.

Let us come close to the Father now in our prayers.
Let us pray.

Prayers

Heavenly Father you are the Father in this story who welcomed home his sons. We thank you that you welcome us home too with great compassion and tender love.
Lord in your mercy, hear our prayer.

Today we come to you as we are with our joys and sorrows, with our fears and anxieties, please hold us in your loving embrace and speak your peace to us.
Lord in your mercy.....

We pray for all those known to us who are suffering in anyway in body, mind or spirit, we pray for all those in hospital at this time, please be close to them and touch them with your healing and peace.
Lord in your mercy.....

We pray for all those who care for us here. We thank you for their care and kindness. Please bless them and help them to feel happy in their work.
Lord in your mercy....

We pray for all our loved ones both near and far that you will bless and keep them in your loving care.
Lord in your mercy.....

Let us draw all these prayers together in the words of

The Lord's Prayer.

The Lost Sheep

Picture: The Lost Sheep by The Benedictine Nuns of Turvey Abbey

Welcome and Introduction

Opening Responses:

Leader: Shield us God
With your crook
And your staff
All: **Bring us safely home**

Leader: Guide us God
With your truth
And your goodness
All: **Bring us safely home**

Leader: Encourage us God
With your oil
And your kindness
All: **Bring us safely home**

Leader: Shepherd us God
Walk with us
Always
All: **Bring us safely home**

Hymn: The Lord's my shepherd

Confession:

Leader: Lord forgive us
All: **Lord forgive us and help us.**

Lord Jesus we come before you today just as we are with our strengths and weaknesses, our doubts and fears, our joys and sorrows.

For the times when we have closed ourselves to God and not loved him with all of our heart. Lord forgive us....

For the times when we have closed ourselves to one another and not loved one another fully. Lord forgive us…

May God our Father forgive us and help us to love him and our neighbours that we might grow together as a community of love and faith. **Amen**

Reading: Luke 15: 4-7 The Parable of the Lost Sheep

Talk

Hymn: The King of Love

Prayers:

Leader: Lord in your mercy
All: Hear our prayer

Let us draw all these prayers together in the words of
The Lord's Prayer

All: Our Father who art in Heaven…

Hymn: I will sing the wondrous story

Blessing:
                May Christ the good shepherd
                Enfold you with love,
                Fill you with peace
                And lead you in hope
                To the end of your days.
                And may God bless you
                And keep you
                And hold you in the palm of his hand.

All: The Grace

Talk

Last week, we ate some pancakes on Shrove Tuesday and remembered that it was the beginning of the Lenten season – the 6-week period which is seen a time of preparation for Easter. I brought a lovely picture of the prodigal son coming home to the father. This week we have another home coming, this time as we can see from the picture, it is the lost sheep coming home.

Has anyone here ever lived in the countryside or worked on a farm? Or is anyone here familiar with the habits of sheep? I have a lovely old-fashioned picture here of a farmer feeding his sheep in the snow. Sheep live outside in all weathers. My daughter goes on the bus to school in Coventry every day. And the bus goes the country route through Brinklow and Wolston. Last month in February she was coming home saying she had seen new born lambs out in the fields. But sheep tend to wander off if they see some nice juicy looking grass in the neighbouring field and they can get themselves into all sorts of scrapes. My husband and I were once out for a walk by one of the canals in Rugby one summer evening and we heard a loud bleating coming from the canal and when we looked, a sheep had fallen into the canal and was thrashing about trying to swim. We called the fire brigade and they came with a boat, but had terrible trouble trying to get this very heavy, sodden sheep into the boat. They got completely wet themselves.

We are going to listen to a story that Jesus told about a sheep that got lost.
Luke 15: 4-7

This is the story of Jesus the Good Shepherd. The story tells us that he had 100 sheep in his care and one day as he is rounding up his sheep for the night and counting them as they go into the enclosure he notices that there is one missing. He has only counted 99 sheep. I expect he goes through the whole thing again. It must be difficult to count sheep because they are always moving and they all look alike. But Jesus knows each one by name and can recognise them all as individuals. He knows which one is missing. He feels very concerned about what might have happened to the sheep. It could have got caught in some bushes. It could have fallen into a pond or a canal, it could be hurt, it could have been attacked by a wild animal. So, he makes the decision to leave the rest of the sheep behind and go off to look for the lost one.

We know that Jesus looks long and hard for the sheep, all the time calling its name, until at last he hears a faint but familiar bleating. At last he has found his sheep. He puts it up onto his shoulders and carries it home. We can see him in the picture here, waving to us and saying, "Look who I've found!" The story goes that the Shepherd was so happy to have found his sheep that he throws a party for his friends and neighbours to celebrate. It made me wonder if the fireman in my story has gone back to the fire station to get dry and had thrown a party to celebrate that they had managed to rescue the sheep from drowning!

So, what does this all mean for us here? Well there are probably about 100 of us here if we include all the residents and staff and just as in the story Jesus knows us all by name. He loves and cares for each of us. From day to day he knows what is happening in our lives. He knows when we wander off, when we feel lost and afraid and alone. He knows when we are in trouble and when we feel far from home. Like the sheep in the story, all we have to do is to call his name. A simple prayer like 'Jesus help me.' Is enough. He is already coming for us and he will hear us calling and come and rescue us and carry us home.

We are not forgotten, we are never alone. Jesus the Good Shepherd is very near. Our next hymn is all about Jesus the Good shepherd the third verse goes: 'Perverse and foolish oft I strayed, but yet in love he sought me, and on his shoulder gently laid and home rejoicing brought me.'

Hymn: The king of love

Prayers

Let us remember that Jesus the Good Shepherd is very close to us as we come to our prayers. Let us pray.

Lord Jesus we thank you that you are our shepherd and that you have been leading and guiding us and providing for us through out our lives. Lord in your mercy....

We pray for all those who are feeling lost and afraid and far from home. May they be comforted by your presence close to them and by the love of all those who support and care for them. Lord in your mercy....

We pray for all those in management here that you would give them your wisdom and guidance in their work. We pray for all those who care for us here, staff and volunteers that you would bless them in their work and fill them with patience, gentleness and love. Lord in your mercy...

We pray for all those known to us who are suffering in anyway in body, mind or spirit. May they be comforted and know your healing and peace. Lord in your mercy.....

Let us draw all these prayers together in the words of
The Lord's Prayer

Song: I will tell the wondrous story
or He's got the whole world – the song they sang at the party.

We can make up our own verse.....
He's got the little lost sheep in his hands

Zacchaeus

Picture:	Zacchaeus - by The Benedictine Nuns of Turvey Abbey
Visual display:	Money bags with chocolate coins inside

Welcome and Introduction

Leader:	We come as ourselves We come as we are
All:	**God welcomes us home**
Leader:	Wherever we have been Whatever we have done
All:	**God welcomes us home**
Leader:	Lost and afraid Found and rejoicing
All:	**God welcomes us home**
Hymn:	Dear Lord and Father

Confession:

Leader:	Lord forgive us
All:	**Lord forgive us and help us.**

Lord Jesus we come before you today just as we are with our strengths and weaknesses, our doubts and fears, our joys and sorrows.

For the times when we have closed ourselves to God and not loved him with all of our heart. Lord forgive us....

For the times when we have closed ourselves to one another and not loved one another fully. Lord forgive us...

May God our Father forgive us and help us to love him and our neighbours that we might grow together as a community of love and faith. **Amen**

Reading:	Luke 19: 1-10

Talk

Hymn:	Come let us sing of a wonderful love

Prayers:

Leader:	Lord in your mercy
All:	**Hear our prayer**

Let us draw all these prayers together in the words of The Lord's Prayer

All:	**Our Father who art in Heaven…**

Hymn:	Just as I am

Blessing:

May the Father bless us, for he has adopted us as his children. May the Son come to help us, for he has received us as brothers and sisters. May the Spirit be with us, for he has made us his dwelling place.

All:	**The Grace**

Talk

This is the story of Zacchaeus the tax collector. As we know at the time of Jesus, Israel was occupied by the Romans and Zacchaeus was employed by the them to collect taxes from the people to give to Rome. I don't think that tax collectors have ever been very popular people, but tax collectors at that time were especially despised and hated because they were helping the enemy. The Roman authorities used them to take money from the people and had no respect for them, but worse than that tax collectors tended to be rich because not only did they take money from the people on behalf of the Romans, but they took extra for themselves. Rome knew they were doing it but turned a blind eye.

Zacchaeus was one of them. He was rich because he had been stealing from the people, but also, he was lonely because of what he had done he was hated by everyone. They called him a 'sinner'. Of course, we are all sinners, but the people viewed Zacchaeus as a much worse sinner than everyone else because he was dishonest, a cheat, a supporter of the enemy.

Zacchaeus had heard about Jesus, about his teaching, his healing and miracles – everyone was talking about him. So, when he hears that Jesus is travelling near to where he lives he is curious to go and see him and find out what sort of man he is. As he approaches the road where Jesus will be walking he sees a huge crowd all gathered straining to see Jesus. Poor Zacchaeus is a very short man and can't see a thing, so he runs on ahead of the crowd and climbs a Sycamore tree, so he can get a better view.

Here in the picture is Zacchaeus in the tree. Can you see the expression on his face? Doesn't he look like he can't believe his eyes. What is going on......?

Jesus has stopped right under the tree and is talking to Zacchaeus. In this picture we can't see Jesus, but clearly Zacchaeus is so surprised that Jesus would stop and talk to him. He is even more surprised when Jesus invites himself to come for dinner at his house. Why do you think that would be so surprising for Zacchaeus...? Well it is because Zacchaeus has no friends. Everyone hates him. No one will talk to him. No one would come into his home, no one would invite him to their home. He has been completely rejected by all who know him. He is their enemy. So, when Jesus treats him as a friend it really is extraordinary.

Something profound happens to Zacchaeus. Firstly, he welcomes Jesus into his home. We don't know what was said between them, but we can only guess that he realises his wrong doing and becomes very, very sorry for all the harm he has caused. He experiences what it is to be forgiven. The burden of guilt and the terrible rejection he has suffered is lifted from him. It is what we call repentance. Repentance is a word that means we have been living our life in a certain way- a way that is far from God and his ways and then we come to realise this and completely change direction so that now instead of living without God we now live for him. And this is what happened to Zacchaeus. At the beginning of the story he was living a very dishonest life which was hurting other people. He was making other people poor so that he could be rich. But now he had met Jesus and he discovers what it meant to welcome God into his home and his life. Jesus is now his friend, and this completely changes his life. But Zacchaeus realises that he has got to put things right. I find this part of the story so beautiful.....Zacchaeus goes to see all the people he has stolen money from and gives the money back, more than that he gives them more than he took to show that he really is sorry and he really has changed.

Can you imagine what it would have been like to hear a knock on your front door, to open the door and see Zacchaeus on the doorstep? How might you feel to see your enemy standing there?. What do you think you might say........? I think there might have been some rather offensive things said, but here is Zacchaeus humbly saying sorry for what he has done and handing over the money he has stolen.
(*Say sorry and hand out the chocolate money to residents in the service see what happens and pick up on peoples' responses.*)

Every week at the beginning of our service we have a time of confession and this is a quiet moment in the service where we can repent. We can take a moment to realise that we have been going in the wrong direction, we haven't always been living for God and following his ways. We all are sinners and we need these times when we do say sorry to God and to one another.

For some of you who have not really met Jesus before, he is here waiting for you like Zacchaeus to welcome him into you home and your life. If you would like to know more about how to welcome Jesus into your life and become his friend, then speak to one of the team afterwards and we will be happy to help you.

Prayers

As we come to our time of prayer, we give thanks that Jesus has come to our home, that he is here with us and wants to be our friend.

Lord Jesus, we know the truth that we are all sinners and just like Zacchaeus we need to repent and turn our lives back to you. Help us to open our hearts and lives to you. We thank you for your forgiveness and love.
Lord in your mercy.....

We pray for all people who have never heard how much God loves them and who don't know that they can be forgiven and become a friend of Jesus. We pray that they will come to know your love and peace.
Lord in you mercy.....

We pray for all those who care for us- for the staff and volunteers and our friends and families, may they experience your tender love at work in their lives.
Lord in your mercy.....

We pray for all those who are unwell or in hospital and all those who are suffering, please give them your strength and comfort.
Lord in your mercy.....

The Lord's Prayer

St Patrick's Day

Visual display: A shamrock

Welcome and Introduction

Opening Responses:

Leader:	Young and old Friends and strangers
All:	**God welcomes us**
Leader:	Lost and bewildered Found and rejoicing
All:	**God welcomes us**
Leader:	This morning, this day This night, for ever
All:	**God welcomes us**

Hymn: Be thou my vision

Confession:

Leader:	Lord forgive us
All:	**Lord forgive us and help us.**

Lord Jesus we come before you today just as we are with our strengths and weaknesses, our doubts and fears, our joys and sorrows.

For the times when we have closed ourselves to God and not loved him with all of our heart. Lord forgive us….

For the times when we have closed ourselves to one another and not loved one another fully. Lord forgive us…

May God our Father forgive us and help us to love him and our neighbours that we might grow together as a community of love and faith. **Amen**

Reading:	Luke 19: 1-10
Talk	

Hymn: I cannot tell (Tune -Danny Boy)

Prayers:

Leader:	Lord in your mercy
All:	**Hear our prayer**

Let us draw all these prayers together in the words of
The Lord's Prayer

All: **Our Father who art in Heaven…**

Blessing: Sung (Tune – Morning has broken)

Christ be beside me, Christ be before me,
Christ be behind me, King of my heart.
Christ be within me, Christ be below me,
Christ be above me, never to part.

Christ on my right hand, Christ on my left hand,
Christ all around me, shield in the strife.
Christ in my sleeping, Christ in my sitting,
Christ in my rising, light of my life.

Christ be in all hearts, thinking about me,
Christ be in all tongues telling of me.
Christ be the vision in eyes that see me,
In ears that hear me, Christ ever be.

All: **The Grace**

Introduction to the service

Today we are celebrating St. Patrick's Day – the patron saint of Ireland.
Although St. Patrick lived a very long time ago during Roman times, there are some beautiful prayers which have been passed down through generations and are still used by the church today. Two of the hymns we will sing in our service today are prayers of St. Patrick set to music.

Talk

St. Patrick is the patron saint of Ireland
He was born in 385 – so long ago during Roman times.
At the time Ireland was a land of pagans and druids.
At the age of 14 Patrick was captured by Irish pirates and taken as a slave to Ireland. He worked there as a shepherd for 6 years.

During this time somehow, God met with him. As he worked away quietly on his own, he began to pray. He was converted and became a Christian.

After 6 years as a slave, when he was about 20 years old he heard a voice telling him that it was time to go home and that a boat was waiting for him. So, he managed to escape and travelled about 20 miles to get to the port and then persuaded the captain to take him back to England. It was three days on the boat and then 28 days walking before he finally arrived home worn out and faint with hunger and was reunited with his family.

A few years later Patrick had a vision where he heard the people of Ireland as with one voice calling him to come back to Ireland. It was this vision that prompted him to become a priest and then later to go back to Ireland as a Christian missionary.

It wasn't all plain sailing, as these were dangerous times and there were druids who were out to kill him, but Patrick was fearless and continued to preach the gospel. There are many prayers written by him where he prays for God's protection conscious that his life is in danger. Thousands of people became Christians through him and he built many churches all over Ireland until his death in 461.

Often people dress in green and wear shamrocks for St. Patrick's Day....
This is because Patrick used the shamrock to explain the Holy Trinity to the pagans. One God but three persons.

Hymn: I cannot tell – to the Irish melody The Londonderry Air/ Danny Boy

Prayers:

As we come to our time of prayer today, like St. Patrick we pray for God's protection over us and all those whom we love.

Heavenly Father we thank you for the example that St. Patrick is for us. Thank you that he heard and answered your call to go to Ireland. Thank you that you protected him from all harm.

We pray that you would be close to all of us here. Please look after us, keep us well and be with us each moment. Lord in your mercy....

We pray that you would bless and keep our families, friends and loved ones safe in your loving care. Lord in your mercy.....

We pray for all those who care for us, for the managers, care staff and volunteers that you would bless and protect and guide them in their work. Lord in your mercy.....

A Prayer of St. Patrick

May God shield us
May God fill us
May God keep us
May God watch over us
May God bring us this day
to the nearness of his love

Let us draw all these
prayers together in
the words of

The Lord's Prayer.

Thanksgiving For Mothers

Picture: Mary and Elisabeth by The Benedictine Nuns of
Turvey Abbey

Welcome and Introduction:

"When Israel was a child, I loved him…It was I who taught Ephraim to walk, taking them by the arms, but they did not realise it was I who healed them. I led them with cords of human kindness, with ties of love." (Hosea 11: 1-4)

Opening Responses:

Leader: Secure on a rock
You gather us
All: **You wrap us round in love**

Leader: Under your wings
You gather us
All: **You wrap us round in love**

Leader: Safe in your house
You gather us in
All: **You wrap us round in love**

Hymn: All things bright and beautiful

Confession

Leader: Lord forgive us
All: **Lord forgive us and help us.**
Lord Jesus we come before you today just as we are with our strengths and weaknesses, our doubts and fears, our joys and sorrows.

For the times when we have closed ourselves to God and not loved him with all of our heart. Lord forgive us….

For the times when we have closed ourselves to one another and not loved one another fully. Lord forgive us…

May God our Father forgive us and help us to love him and our neighbours that we might grow together as a community of love and faith. **Amen**

Reading: Luke 1:39-45

Talk

Hymn: Now thank we all our God

Prayers:

Leader: Lord in your mercy
All: **Hear our prayer**

Let us draw all these prayers together in the words of
The Lord's Prayer

All: **Our Father who art in Heaven…..**

Hymn: He's got the whole world in his hands

Blessing

'Can a mother forget the baby at her breast? And have no compassion on the child she has borne? Though she may forget, I will never forget you. See I have engraved you on the palms of my hands.' So may God bless us and keep us and hold us in the palm of his hand. (Is 49:15-16)

All: **The Grace**

Introduction to the service

Last Sunday (or next Sunday) was (is) Mothering Sunday. Some of us here today are mothers and grandmothers, but all of us have had a mother so today we have a special service of thanksgiving for our mothers and grandmothers and all those who have cared for us and nurtured us, and we will pray for our own children and grandchildren and all those we have had the privilege to care for and nurture. We usually think of God as our Father but there are some beautiful scriptures which show that God also loves us like a mother. Here is one of those scriptures: Hosea 11: 1-4

Talk

This is the story of two special mothers who were also cousins.
The older one is Elisabeth the mother of John the Baptist. The younger one is Mary the mother of Jesus, God's son. Both women were told by an angel that they would bear a son and that their children were especially chosen and called by God for a particular mission in this world. So it was quite a responsibility. Their mothering role was very important. They were called to care for these children, to bring them up in a godly home so that they would know God and be open to his call when it came. They then had to help their children to respond to God's call. It can be hard for mothers to let go of their children and I'm sure that Mary and Elisabeth did find it hard but ultimately they had to let their grown up sons go and do what God had called them to do.

Today as we think about Mothering Sunday I would like us to take time to think about all those special people in our lives. It may be our mothers and grandmothers, but also there will be others who have also loved us, nurtured us, been there for us, supported and encouraged us in our lives.
Would any of you like to tell us about a special person in your life…….

Also I would like us to give thanks for all the opportunities we have had to care for and nurture others. In this room there are mothers and fathers, grandmothers and grandfathers, God-mothers, brothers and sisters and aunts and uncles and neighbours who have been a nurturing, caring and encouraging presence in the lives of others. Some of you may have been Sunday school teachers or youth leaders or been involved in groups like the Girl Guides or Boy Scouts where you have encouraged children and young people to grow and develop.

Let us give thanks today for all those who have touched our lives in a special way, for all that we have given and received from our loved ones.

Prayers

Heavenly Father as we think about Mothering Sunday we thank you for the loving care of our own mothers and grandmothers. Lord in your mercy, hear our prayer.

We also thank you for all those who in our lives have nurtured and supported us, encouraged and inspired us and helped us to grow in faith. Lord in your mercy…..

We pray for your blessing on all those who care for us here. May they serve us with your loving kindness and compassion, your gentleness and patience. Lord in your mercy…..

We pray for our own families, for children and grandchildren, nieces and nephews and God-children that you will keep them all in your loving care. Please bless them with good health and happiness and help them to know that you are ever near. Lord in your mercy…..

We pray for those who have no one to care for them, for those who are alone, orphaned or homeless, may they experience your love and care for them through the love and care of your people. Lord in your mercy….

Let us draw all these prayers together in the words of
The Lord's Prayer

God's Workmanship

Visual display - Example's of residents' art work or handicrafts

Welcome and Introduction

For we are God's workmanship, created in Christ Jesus to do good works, which God prepared in advance for us to do. (Eph 2:10)

Opening Responses:

Leader: God on the road
                 God in the wilderness
All: **God making all things new**

Leader: God in our tears
                 God in our laughter
All: **God making all things new**

Leader: God in our living
                 God in our dying
All: **God making all things new**

Hymn: Great is thy faithfulness

Confession:
Leader: Lord forgive us
All: **Lord forgive us and help us.**

Lord Jesus we come before you today just as we are with our strengths and weaknesses, our doubts and fears, our joys and sorrows.

For the times when we have closed ourselves to God and not loved him with all our heart. Lord forgive us….

For the times when we have closed ourselves to one another and not loved one another fully. Lord forgive us...

May God our Father forgive us and help us to love him and our neighbours that we might grow together as a community of love and faith. **Amen**

Reading: Jer 18: 1- 6, Eph 2: 10

Talk

Hymn: O love that wilt not let me go

Prayers:

Leader: Lord in your mercy
All: **Hear our prayer**

Let us draw all these prayers together in the words of The Lord's Prayer

All: **Our Father who art in Heaven.....**

Hymn: Amazing Grace

Blessing:

'   I thank my God every time I remember you. In all my prayers for all of you, I always pray with joy because of your partnership in the gospel from the first day until now, being confident of this, that he who began a good work in you will carry it on to completion until the day of Christ Jesus.' (Phil 1:3-6) And so, may God bless us and keep us and continue to mould us into the beautiful works of art that we are. **Amen**

All: **The Grace**

Talk

Our scripture today tells us that we are God's workmanship – we are his work of art. Have you ever thought of yourself as a work of art before? You may not have, but some of you here are artists and I have some works of art here that some of you have made for us to look at.

Jer 18: 1-6

This passage describes how God speaks to Jeremiah through watching a potter at work. The potter who is moulding pots and working at the wheel and at some point, the pot becomes a bit misshapen, but it doesn't matter because the potter just starts again and re-moulds the pot. It is like a parable which tells us that this is what God is doing in our lives. He spends the whole of our lives moulding us into the most beautiful works of art. How does he do this? Well he uses the circumstances of our lives both good and bad to shape us. Some of you may have heard it said that our lives are like a beautiful tapestry which God is weaving. The tapestry has both bright threads and dark threads, because both the good times and the more difficult times make up the whole picture of our lives, both are needed to make the tapestry beautiful.
It maybe that as you look back over your lives that you can see now how something that may have seemed dreadful at the time in fact has made you in the long term into a better or a more compassionate person.

Even here in this care home, God is using the daily experiences of our lives here to shape us and to make us more beautiful. Sometimes we rub each other up the wrong way – but it may be that God is making us more patient or understanding with others we really don't like. It can take courage to reach out in friendship to people we don't know very well or to help someone new to feel welcome and part of the community, but if we do reach out in friendship and care for others we will become better, more beautiful people.

We know that works of art say something about the artist, they reflect the artist. We are God's works of art and others who look at us or spend time with us, should be able to see something of God in us, to know what God is like. Most importantly they should be able to experience God's love for them through us. Let's think about that now as we come to our time of prayer:

Prayers

Lord God you are the potter, we are the clay. You are the master craftsman and we are your works of art. May we humbly allow you to mould us and make us into the people you want us to be, people who reflect your beauty. Lord in your mercy.....

All of us have been through many ups and downs in our lives. We thank you Lord that you have been weaving both bright and dark threads into the tapestries of our lives, using these experiences to make us beautiful for you. Lord in your mercy.....

We pray Lord that you would be in the centre of our life together here and that together we would become a community of people that love and serve and care for one another and so doing reflect your love for us. Lord in your mercy......

We pray for all who care for us here. Please be with our managers – give them your wisdom and guidance as they take us forward. Please bless all our carers and volunteers, may they be filled with your love and compassion. Lord in your mercy.....

We pray for all those who suffer in anyway in body, mind and spirit that they may feel you close to them and experience your love through your people. Lord in your mercy......

Let us draw all these prayers together in the words of
The Lord's Prayer.

The Raising of Lazarus

Visual display: A white sheet draped over a table to symbolise a tomb

Welcome and introduction

"I am the resurrection and the life. He who believes in me will live, even though he dies and whoever lives and believes in me will never die." (John 11: 25-26)

Opening responses:

Leader:	In my living and in my loving
All:	**You have blessed me**
Leader:	In my tears and in my laughter
All:	**You have blessed me**
Leader:	In my sisters and in my brothers
All:	**You have blessed me**
Leader:	With everything that's in me
Leader:	I give you thanks
Hymn:	To God be the glory

Confession:

Leader:	Lord forgive us
All:	**Lord forgive us and help us.**

Lord Jesus we come before you today just as we are with our strengths and weaknesses, our doubts and fears, our joys and sorrows.

For the times when we have closed ourselves to God and not loved him with all of our heart. Lord forgive us….

For the times when we have closed ourselves to one another and not loved one another fully. Lord forgive us…

May God our Father forgive us and help us to love him and our neighbours that we might grow together as a community of love and faith. **Amen**

Dramatic reading and
acting from: John 11: 17-44

Talk

Hymn: I am the bread of life (verses 1, 4, 5)

Prayers:

Leader: Lord in your mercy
All: **Hear our prayer**

Let us draw all these prayers together in the words of
The Lord's Prayer

All: **Our Father who art in Heaven…**

Hymn: And can it be

Blessing: God the Father, by whose love Christ was raised from the dead, open to you who believe the gates of everlasting life. **Amen**

God the Son, who in bursting the grave has won a glorious victory, give you joy as you share the Easter faith. **Amen**

God the Holy Spirit, whom the risen Lord breathed into his disciples, empower you and fill you with Christ's peace. **Amen**

All: **The Grace**

Dramatic reading: John 11: 17-44

Stage directions: *Set up a table to one side of the front of the room draped with a white sheet to symbolise a tomb.*

Narrator:
Lazarus, Martha and Mary were a brother and two sisters who lived in Bethany. Bethany is a village only about two miles from Jerusalem. They were great friends of Jesus and he would often visit them and stay with them when he was travelling too and from Jerusalem. At the beginning of this story we hear that Lazarus has become very sick and his two sisters send a message to Jesus to let him know. They are hoping that he will come and heal Lazarus. However, strangely, Jesus makes the decision to delay going to them and waits another two days. When Jesus does eventually get there, Lazarus has already died and has been in the tomb for four days. The two sisters are stricken with grief and lots of neighbours and friends have come to comfort them. When Martha hears that Jesus is coming she goes out to meet him, but Mary stays at home……

Martha: "Lord, if you had only been here, my brother would not have died. But I know that even now God will give you whatever you ask."

Jesus: "Your brother will rise again."

Martha: "I know he will rise again in the resurrection at the last day."

Jesus: "I am the resurrection and the life. He who believes in me will live, even though he dies; and whoever lives and believes in me will never die. Do you believe this?"

Martha: "Yes Lord, I believe that you are the Christ, the son of God who has come into the world."

Narrator: After this Martha went back into the house and called her sister Mary aside.

Martha: "The teacher is here, and he is asking for you."

Narrator: When Mary hears this, she gets up quickly and goes to the place where Jesus was. When she sees him she falls at his feet.

Mary: "Lord, if you had been here, my brother would not have died."

Narrator: When Jesus sees her weeping, he is deeply moved and troubled.

Jesus: "Where have you laid him?"

Martha & Mary: "Come and see Lord"
                "Come and see Lord"

Narrator: Jesus wept.

Jesus: "Take away the stone."

Martha: "But Lord, Lazarus has been in there for four days, there will be a bad odour."

Jesus: "Did I not tell you that if you believed you would see the glory of God?"

Narrator: So, they take away the stone.

Jesus: "Father I thank you that you have heard me. I know that you always hear me, but I say this for the benefit of all those who are standing here that they may believe that you sent me. LAZARUS COME OUT!"

Narrator: The dead man comes out, his hands and feet wrapped with strips of linen, and a cloth around his face.
(Lazarus comes out wearing a sheet over his head and body)

Jesus: "Take off the grave clothes and let him go."
(Mary and Martha pull the sheet off and there is Lazarus alive)

Talk

Well…What a story! This story of the death and raising to life of Lazarus is very significant because it comes not long before Jesus' own death and resurrection. Somehow these two events are connected.

We see in this story that Jesus delays going to see Lazarus when he is sick because clearly, he is planning something. When Jesus raises Lazarus to life, he wants to say something about his own death and about your death and my death.

As we have heard, Jesus arrives to find Martha and Mary in utter grief over the loss of their brother. Mary is inconsolable and doesn't even come out to see Jesus when he first arrives. Martha is bewildered - "Why didn't you come? If you had been here my brother would not have died. What does this mean? Why didn't you help us when we asked you to?"

These questions are rather like the ones we may have asked when we have lost someone very dear to us and we are full of grief? Where were you God? Why didn't you help us? Why did ….have to die? But despite these questions Martha shows great faith when she says; "But I know even now that God will give you what you ask."

Somehow, I think she knows that this isn't the end of the story. Jesus says to her, "Your brother will rise again." It is a bit like us saying to bereaved people, "He's gone to Heaven, or you will see him again." Martha already knows this, and she says, "Yes, I know he will rise again in the resurrection at the last day." But then Jesus says something very challenging - "I am the resurrection and the life. He who believes in me will live even though he dies and whoever lives and believes in me will never die. **Do you believe this?"**

In fact, this is so challenging because Jesus is saying directly to us, "If you live and believe in me, even though you will die - your life here in the world will come to an end, you will live again.

Just as Lazarus died and has been raised, just as I am going to die and be raised so you also will be raised to new life. He says to Martha and to us, **"Do you believe this?"**

Martha responds in a most wonderful way, "Yes Lord, I believe that you are the Christ, the Son of God who has come into the world."

In a couple of weeks' time we will enter into Holy Week – the final week of Jesus' life.

We will gather around the cross and reflect on his death and then on Easter Sunday we will joyfully celebrate his resurrection. With Martha we will declare, **"Yes Lord we believe that you are the Christ, the Son of God."**

But even more than that we can know in our own heart that when our time comes, our death will not be the end of our story, but we too will be raised to new life.

This is really something to celebrate.

Prayers

As we come now to our time of prayer let us remember Jesus' words to us,

'I am the resurrection and the life. You who believe in me will live even though you die.......Do you believe this?'

Lord Jesus thank you for your wonderful words which give us such hope, please give us your gift of faith so that we may respond like Martha did,

"Yes Lord I believe that you are the Christ the Son of God who has come into the world."

Lord in your mercy...... Hear our prayer

As we are soon to approach Holy Week, we pray that you will help us to enter in to the very heart of our faith. We thank you for coming into our world, for living among us, for dying on the cross so that we could be forgiven for our sin and come to know God as our Father. We thank you for conquering death and rising to new life so that we too can be raised to new life with you.

Lord in your mercy.......Hear our prayer

We pray that you would help us to share the joy of this good news with our friends and families and with all those with whom we live in this home. May they come to know Jesus and the new life he gives.

Lord in your mercy......Hear our prayer

We pray for all those known to us who are sad at the loss of a loved one, may they come to know your comfort and strength in their loss.

Lord in your mercy......Hear our prayer

The Lord's Prayer

Mary of Bethany

Visual display: Perfume bottles, fragrant oil, scented hand cream

Welcome and introduction
Then Mary took about a pint of pure nard, an expensive perfume; she poured it on Jesus' feet and wiped his feet with her hair, and the house was filled with the fragrance of the perfume. (John 12:3)

Opening responses:

Leader:	Shine in our lives Warm us with courage
All:	**Keep us close to you**
Leader:	Shine in our lives Light up our darkness
All:	**Keep us close to you**
Leader:	Shine in our lives Raise us to glory
All:	**Keep us close to you**
Hymn:	Brother, sister let me serve you

Confession:

Leader:	Lord forgive us
All:	**Lord forgive us and help us.**

Lord Jesus we come before you today just as we are with our strengths and weaknesses, our doubts and fears, our joys and sorrows.

For the times when we have closed ourselves to God and not loved him with all of our heart. Lord forgive us....

For the times when we have closed ourselves to one another and not loved one another fully. Lord forgive us...

May God our Father forgive us and help us to love him and our neighbours that we might grow together as a community of love and faith. **Amen**

Reading: John 12: 1-8

Talk

Hymn: Father we adore you

(During this hymn, the chaplain places a little cross of fragrant oil or scented hand cream on the palm of the hands of all those who would like it)

Prayers:
Leader: Lord in your mercy
All: **Hear our prayer**

Let us draw all these prayers together in the words of
The Lord's Prayer

All: **Our Father who art in Heaven…**

Hymn: How sweet the name of Jesus

Blessing: May God give us his comfort and his peace His light and his joy in this world and the next and may God bless us and keep us safe in the palm of his hand. **Amen**

All: **The Grace**

Talk

We find ourselves back in the little home at Bethany – the place where Jesus went to spend time with his friends Lazarus, Mary and Martha. Last week we heard the extraordinary story of Lazarus becoming sick and dying and then Jesus raising him back to life. It was just after this amazing display of power that we read that the religious leaders began a plot to arrest Jesus and put him to death. Jesus is now in the final days or weeks of his life.

Our reading today tells us that Martha and Mary are having a dinner party in Jesus' honour to thank him for raising up Lazarus. Jesus and his disciples are at the table with Lazarus and Martha is serving the meal. Then Mary takes a beautiful bottle of perfume which we are told is worth the equivalent of a whole year's wages – in today's money that would be about £25,000. She opens the bottle and pours the whole lot over Jesus' feet. What an extraordinary thing to do! Imagine the perfume running all over the floor. And so costly! The Bible says that the fragrance of the perfume fills the house. I imagine the smell must have lingered on for days afterwards.

I wonder what they were all thinking? I wonder what you are thinking?
We know what Judas was thinking – his reaction was, 'What a waste!' What a waste of something so precious. What a waste of money – which could have been used to help the poor.
But Jesus defends Mary. He says, 'Leave her alone. This perfume is for my burial.'

So, what does all this mean? Why did Mary pour her precious perfume all over Jesus' feet?
Well, I think that she had been listening carefully to Jesus and she had heard him speaking about his own death. His disciples had also heard this, but they had not really taken it in and even when he was arrested in the garden they were not expecting it and didn't know what to do when it happened. But Mary knew that Jesus was going to die on a cross very soon. I believe that what she did was to express her very great love for Jesus. Pouring out the perfume was an act of worship, of adoration. She gave him all she had. Before he died, Mary wanted him to know how precious he was to her. Her tender love was in such contrast to the brutality Jesus would suffer at the hands of the Romans.

In a moment we are going to sing our next hymn:

Father we adore you lay our lives before you, how we love you

As we sing this song, I am going to come around, and place a little cross of fragrant oil or hand cream on the palm of your hands. This is to remind you that you are very precious to Jesus.
But also, we have now come to the end of our six-week journey through the season of Lent. Next week is Holy Week. We will be walking with Jesus through the last week of his life remembering some important events which are at the heart of our faith especially Jesus' death on the cross and his resurrection to new life on Easter Sunday.

Prayers
As we come now to this time of prayer, may I encourage you to smell the fragrant oil on the palm of your hand and to give thanks that you are precious to Jesus. It can remind you too that Jesus is precious to you. We think of Mary pouring out the precious gift of herself to Jesus in gratitude for all he had done for her.

Lord Jesus, we thank you so much for all you mean to us. We thank you for coming to this world to tell us about God's love for us. We thank you for dying on the cross, so we could be forgiven our sins and come to know God as our Father. We thank you for your promise of new life and eternity with you in Heaven. Lord in your mercy…..Hear our prayer.

Lord Jesus we pray that we would always feel close to you and know how much you love us. Lord in your mercy…..

We pray at this time for all those who are near the end of their lives. Please hold them safe in your loving arms and give them your peace. Lord in your mercy…..

We pray for all those who care for us, for the staff and volunteers and for all our families and friends. May they experience your tender love poured out for them. Lord in your mercy…..
The Lord's Prayer

HOLY WEEK

Holy Week

Introduction

In this section there are services for Palm Sunday, Maundy Thursday and Good Friday. It can be a very moving and enriching experience to re-live Holy Week with our residents in a care home community. However, with the routines of the home and activity programme it may not be possible to celebrate these events on the actual days, so these services can be done on the nearest day available, with the exception of Good Friday which should be on the actual day. It may be possible to have an extra service on Good Friday even if it is not your usual service day especially as you will probably find there are residents who really do want to mark this day. It may not be possible to celebrate all the events of Holy Week, so you may want to have one service and take elements from the different services suggested here.

Holy Week marks the final week of Jesus' life, and is the very heart of our Christian faith. It is a week of dramatic events and mixed emotions which we have tried to capture in pictures, dramatic readings and acting out of the stories as well as in the music we have chosen. We want our residents to feel the exuberant joy as Jesus rides into Jerusalem as the King of the Jews.

We want them to become the friends of Jesus gathered in the upper room to eat a last meal and say "Goodbye" to him. You may want to have a simple communion service together or to have a foot washing service as is suggested here. Ask residents who have the capacity to choose to have their feet washed to take part as well as willing staff, relatives or volunteers. Place their feet in a bowl and pour warm water from a jug over their feet. Dry each person's feet with a fresh towel. The rest of the residents can watch and sing.

On Good Friday we gather around the cross to prayerfully reflect on the death of our Lord. It may be that some of your residents can do some of the readings and prayers. We have suggested you use the poster series called 'The Way of the Cross for Children' which clearly illustrates Jesus' passion in images that are not too violent. These pictures can be purchased from McCrimmons publishers. The atmosphere is reverent and sombre but can finish on a hopeful note because we know that Jesus' death was not the end of the story. You may want to have drinks and hot cross buns together when the service is finished.

Holy Week is a lovely time to do some seasonal Easter activities. You will see some ideas for activities on the following pages.
We have enjoyed making;

Easter gardens	with a stone that can be rolled away on Easter Day
Easter tree	decorated with cardboard crosses and painted eggs.
Cross of flowers	a simple cross loosely wrapped around in chicken wire with oasis inside. Residents can then push flowers into the oasis. We created this cross on Good Friday and used it for our visual display on Easter Sunday.
Hot cross buns	ingredients mixed and baked by the residents and staff.

Planning a Palm Sunday Service

Mood and atmosphere: Exuberant and joyful (and yet remembering that Jesus was soon to die on the cross)

Colours: Purple

Visual display: Picture of Jesus riding on a donkey

A basket of palm crosses

Theme/story/message: Jesus is a humble, servant king

Reading: John 12:12-15

Hymns: Ride on ride on in majesty

All glory laud and honour

Make way, make way by Graham Kendrick

Hosanna by Carl Tuttle

Sing hosanna

The Servant King by Graham Kendrick

The Lord of the Dance

Prayer over the palms:

God our Saviour,
whose Son entered Jerusalem as Messiah to
suffer and die:
May these palms be for us a sign of his victory;
May we who carry them ever hail him as king and
follow him in the way that leads to eternal life.
With all the faithful may we enter the new
Jerusalem in triumph.
In Jesus name.
Amen

Visual aids: A full sized palm
Some clothes or colourful cloths to lay on the floor

Activities or 3D ideas: Make palm crosses out of palm leaves or by decorating crosses made of card which can then be hung with decorated eggs on an Easter tree

105

Palm Sunday

Picture: Jesus riding on a donkey by The Benedictine Nuns of
Turvey Abbey

Welcome and Introduction

Make Way, Make Way – play or sing this song

Opening Responses:

Leader: Hosanna to the Son of David
All: **Hosanna in the highest**

Leader: Blessed is he who comes in the name of the Lord
All: **Hosanna in the highest**

Prayer over the palms:
Let us pray as we hold up our palms

Leader: God our Saviour,
whose Son entered Jerusalem as Messiah to
suffer and die:
May these palms be for us a sign of his victory;
May we who carry them ever hail him as king and
follow him in the way that leads to eternal life.
With all the faithful may we enter the new
Jerusalem in triumph.
In Jesus name.
Amen

Distribute palms

Hymn: Hosanna, hosanna (wave palms)

Confession:

Leader: Lord forgive us
All: **Lord forgive us and help us.**

Lord Jesus we come before you today just as we are with our strengths and weaknesses, our doubts and fears, our joys and sorrows.

For the times when we have closed ourselves to God and not loved him with all of our heart. Lord forgive us….

For the times when we have closed ourselves to one another and not loved one another fully. Lord forgive us…

May God our Father forgive us and help us to love him and our neighbours here that we might continue to grow together as a community of love and faith. **Amen.**

Reading: John 12: 12-15

Talk

Hymn: The Lord of the Dance

Prayers:

Leader: Lord in your mercy
All: **Hear our prayer**

Let us draw all these prayers together in the words of
The Lord's Prayer

All: **Our Father who art in Heaven….**

Hymn: Sing Hosanna

Blessing: Eternal God,
In your tender love towards the human race
you sent your Son our Saviour Jesus Christ
to take our flesh and to suffer death upon a cross.
Grant that we may follow the example of his
great humility, and share in the glory of his
resurrection;
Through Jesus Christ our Lord. **Amen.**

All: **The Grace**

Talk

Palm Sunday is a special day for several reasons;

It is the day we remember Jesus' triumphal entry into Jerusalem. But was it really triumphal? The people of Israel at that time were living under Roman occupation and they would have been used to seeing the triumphal entrances of the Roman centurions on horse back and in chariots dressed in their shining red uniforms. There was nothing of this in the way Jesus entered the city. He was riding a little donkey, wearing his ordinary poor clothes and surrounded by a motley crowd of well wishers- ordinary people, disciples, children waving palms. It all gave the message that Jesus came in peace, not as a military leader to overthrow Rome but as a servant.

We begin what was to be the last week of Jesus' life on earth. This week has become known as Holy Week by the church. It is a week when we celebrate the last meal that Jesus had with his disciples. It was during this meal that Jesus taught his disciples about servant hood and demonstrated what he meant by getting down on his knees and washing his disciples' feet. We will be thinking about this at our service next week. Then Friday is Good Friday. Good Friday is when we remember Jesus' ultimate act of service to us as he gave up his life for us on the cross. Jesus calls us to a life like his own, a life of love and service to God and to one another. The whole story of Easter is summed up in the words of our next song…..

The Lord of the Dance…

Prayers

Let us pray

Lord Jesus we thank you for the ordinary people who welcomed you with such joy into the city of Jerusalem on that first Palm Sunday. May we like them joyfully welcome you into our hearts and lives this Easter time. Lord in your mercy….

Jesus, we thank you that when you came it was not as a military power to over throw the Romans, but you came in the power of love and in humility to serve and to give your life for the world. Lord in your mercy….

We pray that you would help us to follow your example in our daily lives. Help us to stay close to you and to be channels of your loving service to all those with whom we live and come into contact. Lord in your mercy….

We thank you for all those who serve us here. Please fill them with your tender love and compassion and bless them and their families. Lord in your mercy…..

We pray for all those known to us who are suffering in anyway in body, mind and spirit and all those in hospital at this time, may they know your healing touch and your peace. Lord in your mercy…..

Let us draw all these prayers together in the words of
The Lord's Prayer.

109

Planning The Last Supper

Mood and atmosphere: An intimate gathering of Jesus' closest friends

Colours: **Purple**

Visual display: Picture - Jesus washes Peter's feet, a bowl, jug of warm water, towel

Theme/story/message:

Jesus washes his disciples feet. He wants us to be servants to one another

Reading: John 13: 1-15

Hymns: The Servant King by Graham Kendrick

Brother, sister let me serve you by Richard Gillard

Make me a channel of your peace by Sebastian Temple

A new commandment I give unto you

Prayers:

Leader: Gracious God, In the upper room, gathered with his disciples, your Son Jesus Christ girded himself with a towel and washed their feet. Give us the will to be the servants of others as he was the servant of all. Lord in your mercy…

All: **Hear our prayer**

Leader: In the upper room, Jesus prayed for his disciples to be one. We pray for the unity of your Church and ask that we your people here may also be one.
Lord in your mercy….

All: **Hear our prayer**

Leader: In the upper room, Jesus commanded his disciples to love one another. We pray for all those who feel rejected, unloved or lonely that they may be drawn into the fellowship of God's family. Lord in your mercy…

All: **Hear our prayer**

Leader: In the upper room, Jesus told his disciples that he was going to prepare a place for them, we remember all our loved ones who have gone before us and give thanks for the hope we have that we will one day inherit with them eternal life.
Lord in your mercy…

All: **Hear our prayer**

Visual aids: Chaplain washes the feet of those who would like to participate, residents who can give consent, staff, volunteers, relatives. Use a clean towel for each person. Alternatively put a little cross of fragrant hand cream on residents' hands.

The Last Supper

Picture: Jesus washes the feet of Peter by The Benedictine
Nuns of Turvey Abbey

Welcome and Introduction

"A new commandment I give to you that you love one another as I have loved you. By this shall all men know that you are my disciples if you love one another."

Opening responses:

Leader:	Holy God
	Rich in mercy
All:	**Bless us with love**
Leader:	Healing God
	Firm in forgiveness
All:	**Bless us with love**
Leader:	Servant God
	Giving your life for us
All:	**Bless us with love**

Hymn: The Servant King

Confession:

Leader:	Lord forgive us
All:	**Lord forgive us and help us.**

Lord Jesus we come before you today just as we are with our strengths and weaknesses, our doubts and fears, our joys and sorrows.

For the times when we have closed ourselves to God and not loved him with all our heart. Lord forgive us….

For the times when we have closed ourselves to one another and not loved one another fully. Lord forgive us…

May God our Father forgive us and help us to love him and our neighbours, that we might continue to grow together as a community of love and faith. **Amen**

Reading: John 13:1-15

Talk and washing of the feet:
[or instead of foot washing put a little cross of fragrant hand cream on the palm of residents hands]

Hymn: Brother, sister let me serve you – sung while the chaplain washes the feet of those who have agreed to have their feet washed.

Prayers:

We draw all these prayers together in the words of
The Lord's Prayer

All: **Our Father who art in Heaven….**

Hymn: Make me a channel of your peace

Blessing
                   Eternal God,
                   In your tender love towards the human race
                   You sent your Son our Saviour Jesus Christ
                   To take our flesh and to suffer death upon the cross.
                   Grant that we may follow the example of his humility,
                   And share in the glory of his resurrection;
                   Through Jesus Christ our Lord. Amen

                   And may God bless us and keep us and hold us in the palm of his hand.

All: **The Grace**

Talk

Here we are gathered together as Jesus' disciples today in this room, very much like those first disciples. These beautiful pictures show Jesus and his disciples sitting around a table to share the Passover meal.

The passage we have just read describes a most extraordinary event. In those days in Israel which was a hot, dry and dusty place, people wore open sandals. As they walked about their feet became caked in dust and mud. It was the job of the lowliest of servants in the household to wash people's dirty feet before they sat down to eat a meal. So, it was a surprising and confusing thing for the disciples when Jesus took the place of that lowliest servant and began to wash their feet. If you remember that this was the last time that they would all be together with Jesus before his arrest, it was the last meal they would eat together. It would have been a special, rather intimate time. I imagine Jesus moving around the table to each one in turn and as he washed their feet he perhaps had a word of encouragement, of blessing for each one, perhaps a last word before he died. It would have been very moving I think.

Washing of the feet.

Jesus chose to do this act of service as a way of showing his disciples then and us now what it means to follow him and how he wants us to live. He was really saying that he wants it to be a way of life for us to serve others in this way.

I have chosen our next hymn because I think it describes so beautifully what it means to live this life of service. It involves both serving others and allowing others to serve us, so that we are able to both give and receive love. It involves reaching out to others who are suffering, holding a hand or speaking a kind word. It involves sharing the joys and sorrows of those around us, showing care and compassion. There are so many opportunities here for us to serve one another. Little acts of kindness go a long way. Let us think about that as we sing this song together.

Brother, sister let me serve you.

Prayers

Leader: Gracious God, In the upper room, gathered with his disciples, your Son Jesus Christ girded himself with a towel and washed their feet. Give us the will to be the servants of others as he was the servant of all.
Lord in your mercy
All: **Hear our prayer**

Leader: In the upper room, Jesus prayed for his disciples to be one. We pray for the unity of your Church and ask that we your people here may also be one.
Lord in your mercy
All: **Hear our prayer**

Leader: In the upper room, Jesus commanded his disciples to love one another. We pray for all those who feel rejected, unloved or lonely that they may be drawn into the fellowship of God's family.
Lord in your mercy
All: **Hear our prayer**

Leader: In the upper room, Jesus told his disciples that he was going to prepare a place for them, we remember all our loved ones who have gone before us and give thanks for the hope we have that we will one day inherit with them eternal life.
Lord in your mercy
All: **Hear our prayer**

Planning Good Friday

Mood and atmosphere: Sombre, reverent, beautiful, prayerful

Colours: Purple

Visual display: Pictures depicting the way of the cross
                      'The Way of the Cross for Children'

              1. Jesus prays in the Garden of Gethsemane

              2. Jesus is arrested

              3. Jesus is tried

              4. Jesus is crucified

              5. Jesus is buried

Theme/ story/ message: Jesus died on the cross

Bible reading: Simplified readings are included

Hymns: There is a green hill

              Abide with me

              When I survey

              Man of sorrows

              Were you there when they crucified my Lord

              Jesus remember me- Taize

              The Lord of the dance

              The old rugged cross

Visual aids: A cross made of flowers (see example given)

              constructed before,during or after the service.

              An Easter garden with the stone rolled in front of the tomb

Activities and 3D ideas:

Making and sharing hot cross buns

Good Friday

Pictures: The Way of the Cross for Children - poster set

Welcome and Introduction

Reading:
All: **For God so loved the world that he gave his only Son, Jesus Christ, that whoever believes in him shall not perish but have eternal life.**

Hymn: There is a green hill

Picture and reading: <u>Jesus prays in the Garden of Gethsemane</u>

Leader: In this time of great distress and suffering, Jesus asks his disciples to stay awake, to watch and pray and to support him in his time of suffering. May we always stay close to Jesus.

Lord Jesus may we always be mindful of those around us who suffer, may we support and serve one another with kindness and prayer. Lord in your mercy

All: **Hear our prayer**

Hymn: Abide with me

Picture and reading: <u>Jesus is arrested</u>

Leader: Jesus was betrayed by one of his closest friends and yet forgave.

Lord Jesus we too have been hurt and let down by those close to us. And we too have caused offence or hurt others. May we all be forgiven and reconciled to you and to one another. Lord in your mercy

All: **Hear our prayer** 119

Picture and reading: <u>Jesus is tried</u>

Leader: Jesus suffered injustice, mockery and violence.

           Lord Jesus we pray for all those in our world today
           who are victims of injustice and who are mistreated.
           May the love of God overcome the power of hatred
           and evil. Lord in your mercy

All: Hear our prayer

Hymn: When I survey the wondrous cross

Picture and reading: <u>Jesus is crucified</u>

Leader: At the end of his life the thief turned to Jesus on the
           cross and said "Jesus remember me when you
           come into your kingdom." Jesus reassures the thief
           that he too will be there in paradise.

           Lord Jesus, thank you for the hope we have that
           one day we too will be with you in paradise. Lord in
           your mercy

All: Hear our prayer

Hymn: Jesus remember me when you come into your
           kingdom (Taize)

Silence: Let us take a few moments for silent reflection

Picture and reading: <u>Jesus is buried</u>

Leader: Jesus died, and his body was taken down and laid in the tomb. But this was not the end of the story. We look forward with joy to celebrating his resurrection on Sunday. And we give thanks that his story continues in us. We now have become witnesses of his death and resurrection and he lives in us. Let us rejoice as we sing together our final hymn.

Hymn: The Lord of the dance

Final Prayer

Leader: Eternal God, In your tender love towards the human race. You sent your Son our Saviour Jesus Christ to take our flesh and to suffer death upon the cross. Grant that we may follow the example of his humility, and share in the glory of his resurrection;
Through Jesus Christ our Lord. Amen
May God bless us and keep us and hold us in the palm of his hand.

All: The Grace

Jesus Prays in the Garden

They came to a place called Gethsemane, and Jesus said to his disciples, "Sit here while I pray." He took Peter, James, and John with him. Distress and anguish came over him, and he said to them, "The sorrow in my heart is so great that it almost crushes me. Stay here and keep watch."
He went a little farther on, threw himself on the ground, and prayed, "Father, all things are possible for you. Take this cup of suffering away from me. Yet not my will but yours be done."

Jesus is Arrested

Jesus was still speaking when Judas, one of the twelve disciples arrived. With him was a crowd armed with swords and clubs and sent by the religious leaders. The traitor had given the crowd a signal: "The man I kiss is the one you want. Arrest him and take him away under guard."
As soon as Judas arrived, he went up to Jesus and said, "Teacher!" and kissed him. So, they arrested Jesus and took him away.

Jesus is Tried

The soldiers first took Jesus to the High Priest's house to be tried by the religious leaders, but because they did not have the power to execute a person, the religious leaders then took Jesus to Pilate the Roman governor. After questioning Jesus, Pilate decided he did not deserve to die. Because he wanted to save Jesus, he offered the crowd a choice. "Every year at Passover, I release one prisoner. This year I can release Barabbas, the murderer, or Jesus. Which would you prefer?" At the urging of their leaders, the crowd shouted for Barabbas. Pilate was surprised. "What then shall I do with Jesus?" He asked. "Crucify him! Crucify him!" They yelled over and over.
Pilate shrugged. He called for a bowl of water and a towel and washed his hands in front of the crowd. "I am not responsible for this man's death," he said. Then he gave orders for Barabbas to be released and for Jesus to be whipped and crucified.
The soldiers took Jesus to their barracks. They put a royal robe on him and a crown of thorns on his head. They bowed before him and taunted him, "Hail, King of the Jews!" Then they led him out to be executed.

Jesus Is Crucified

The soldiers took Jesus to a hill named Calvary just outside of Jerusalem to crucify him. They nailed his hands and feet to a wooden cross and placed a sign above his head which said, 'Jesus of Nazareth, King of the Jews.' Two robbers were crucified with Jesus. The religious leaders came to jeer at Jesus, "If you are God's son, let's see you save yourself now!"
Jesus looked down and said, "Father forgive them. They do not know what they are doing."
One of the robbers joined the crowd taunting Jesus, "If you are God's son, save yourself and save us too!" But the other robber defended Jesus, "Be quiet! We deserve what we are getting. Jesus does not." Then he turned to Jesus and said, "Remember me when you come into your Kingdom." Jesus replied, "Today you will be with me in Paradise."
At noon, a deep darkness fell across the land and lasted until three o'clock. At that time Jesus cried out, "It is finished!" and then, "Into your hands I put my spirit." And then he died.
The captain of the soldiers, who had watched everything said quietly, "Surely this man was the Son of God."

Jesus is Buried

That evening a disciple named Joseph of Arimathea went and asked for Jesus' body. Pilate gave orders for it to be given to him. Joseph took the body and wrapped it in a clean linen cloth. He then placed the body in his own tomb that had been cut into solid rock and had never been used. He rolled a big stone against the entrance of the tomb and went away.

EASTER

Celebrating the Season of Easter
Introduction

The services that follow take us through the appearances of Jesus to his disciples following his resurrection. They are wonderful stories of Jesus alive, risen from the dead. As we live this season with our residents, we are moved from the sadness and suffering of the cross with all its pain and loss to a place of great joy as we realise that death on a cross was not the end of Jesus' story. There will be times when our work with elderly residents will take us to the cross. We are there accompanying people on the final stage of their lives on earth. We are witnesses to times of pain, suffering and loss. However we hold in our hearts the great hope that our faith gives us, that this suffering and loss is not the end of the story. Jesus died and rose again and so will we! This is the message of the Easter Story. The season of Easter which goes on for six weeks up until Pentecost is an opportunity to impart this hope to our residents.

These stories are full of drama and emotion, of faith and hope, of doubt and fear. They lend themselves to being acted out. The following pages contain scripts so that the texts can be read dramatically or adapted for acting. We have often included our residents in the acting and made them the disciples hiding behind locked doors, or the disciples hearing the news from the women that they have seen the Lord, or the disciples who went fishing with Peter and then were invited to breakfast on the beach with Jesus. In our experience residents have been drawn into the drama and have had their own encounters with Jesus as we have told the stories in this way.

Planning Easter Services

Mood and atmosphere: Joyful and celebratory

Colours: White and gold

Visual displays: Pictures depicting Jesus' appearances after his resurrection

Easter Garden with the stone rolled away

Daffodils and other spring flowers

Theme/ story/ message: Jesus is alive!

Telling the stories of Jesus meeting with his disciples after his resurrection and his ascension after 40 days.

We are an Easter People, the People of the Resurrection

Bible readings: Matthew 28, Mark 16, Luke 24, John 20, 21

Hymns: Jesus Christ is risen today (Christ the Lord is risen today)

Thine be the glory

Crown him with many crowns

Alleluia, alleluia give thanks to the risen Lord

Be still for the presence of the Lord

Thank you Jesus, thank you Lord for loving me

Alleluia, sing to Jesus

Spirit of the living God

Sharing the Peace: When Jesus met his disciples after his resurrection he often greets them with the words of the Peace and so these words have been incorporated into the following services and allow time for greeting one another.

Visual Aids: Empty cross with white drape

Cross of flowers

Activities and 3D ideas: The Easter readings lend themselves to story telling, dramatic reading and acting.

127

Easter Sunday
Meeting Jesus in the garden

Visual Display: An Easter garden, Easter tree, model of the garden tomb

Welcome and Introduction

Opening response:

Leader: Alleluia! Christ is risen!
All: **He is risen indeed**
              Alleluia!

'Let us fix our eyes on Jesus, the author and perfecter of our faith, who for the joy set before him endured the cross, scorning its shame, and sat down at the right hand of the throne of God.' (Heb 12:2)

Hymn: Jesus Christ is risen today

Confession:

Leader: Lord forgive us
All: **Lord forgive us and help us.**

Lord Jesus we come before you today just as we are with our strengths and weaknesses, our doubts and fears, our joys and sorrows.

For the times when we have closed ourselves to God and not loved him with all our heart. Lord forgive us....

For the times when we have closed ourselves to one another and not loved one another fully. Lord forgive us...

May God our Father forgive us and help us to love him and our neighbours, that we might continue to grow together as a community of love and faith. **Amen**

Dramatic Reading: John 20 v 1-18

Talk:

Hymn: Crown him with many crowns

Prayers:
Leader: Lord in your mercy
All: **Hear our prayer**

Let us draw all these prayers together in the words of
The Lord's Prayer.

All: **Our Father who art in Heaven…..**

The Peace:

Leader: On the evening of the first day of the week,
                         when the disciples were together, Jesus
                         came and stood among them and said,
                         "Peace be with you."
                         The peace of the Lord be always with you.
All: **And also with you**

Hymn: Thine be the glory

Blessing:

                         God the Father,
                         By whose glory Christ was raised from the
                         dead, strengthen us to walk with him in his
                         risen life. And may God bless us, the Father,
                         the Son and the Holy Spirit Amen.

All: **The Grace**

Dramatic Reading: John 20:1-18 (NIV)

The Empty Tomb

20 Early on the first day of the week, while it was still dark, Mary Magdalene went to the tomb and saw that the stone had been removed from the entrance. ² So she came running to Simon Peter and the other disciple, the one Jesus loved, and said,

"They have taken the Lord out of the tomb, and we don't know where they have put him!"

³ So Peter and the other disciple started for the tomb. ⁴ Both were running, but the other disciple outran Peter and reached the tomb first. ⁵ He bent over and looked in at the strips of linen lying there but did not go in. ⁶ Then Simon Peter came along behind him and went straight into the tomb. He saw the strips of linen lying there, ⁷ as well as the cloth that had been wrapped around Jesus' head. The cloth was still lying in its place, separate from the linen. ⁸ Finally the other disciple, who had reached the tomb first, also went inside. He saw and believed. ⁹ (They still did not understand from Scripture that Jesus had to rise from the dead.) ¹⁰ Then the disciples went back to where they were staying.

Jesus appears to Mary Magdalene

¹¹ Now Mary stood outside the tomb crying. As she wept, she bent over to look into the tomb ¹² and saw two angels in white, seated where Jesus' body had been, one at the head and the other at the foot. ¹³ They asked her,

"Woman, why are you crying?"

"They have taken my Lord away, and I don't know where they have put him."

¹⁴ At this, she turned around and saw Jesus standing there, but she did not realise that it was Jesus. ¹⁵ He asked her,

"Woman, why are you crying? Who is it you are looking for?"

Thinking he was the gardener, she said,

"Sir, if you have carried him away, tell me where you have put him, and I will get him."

¹⁶ Jesus said to her,

"Mary."

She turned toward him and cried out in Aramaic,

"Rabboni!"

¹⁷ "Do not hold on to me, for I have not yet ascended to the Father. Go instead to my brothers and tell them, 'I am ascending to my Father and your Father, to my God and your God.'"

¹⁸ Mary Magdalene went to the disciples with the news:

"I have seen the Lord!"

And she told them that he had said these things to her.

Talk

The last time that we were all together like this we were remembering Good Friday. It was a very special atmosphere as we gathered at the cross. I have always had enormous admiration for the women in the story who stood at the foot of the cross on Good Friday and stayed with Jesus as he died. What courage it must have taken to do that. It is hard for us to imagine, but those of you who have nursed a loved one when they were ill or been at the bedside of someone who is dying or watched a loved one suffering will perhaps be able to understand something of what those women went through as they watched Jesus die. Today we follow the story of Mary Magdalene who was one of those women at the cross. She goes early on Sunday morning, with oils and spices to the tomb where Jesus had been laid, intending to embalm his body. We can imagine her grief and sense of loss and then her confusion as she looks into the tomb and realises that Jesus is not there. In fact, she sees two angels who ask her why she is crying, and then a man who she mistakes for the gardener. I do not know why Mary does not recognise Jesus, perhaps she is just too full of grief and through her tears can not see him properly, but there is a very touching moment when Jesus speaks her name; "Mary" and then she recognises him. It's Jesus! She runs off to tell the disciples that she has seen the Lord.

I know that probably most of us here have known what it is to lose people who are very dear to us. Many of us will have suffered a great deal in different ways. We can question what the meaning of this suffering and loss is. For myself the only way I can make any kind of sense of the difficult times in our lives is to think about the resurrection of Jesus. It gives me hope that just as suffering and death were not the end of the story for Jesus, so they won't be the end of our story either. We can hold onto this hope that just as Jesus went through suffering and death and then was raised to new life so have our loved ones who have gone before us. But also, one day when the time is right each one of us will hear Jesus speak our own name. He will call us by name and invite us to be with him in Heaven for ever.

Prayers

Lord Jesus on this Easter Day you come to greet us in the garden. You are the risen Christ and you call each one of us by name. Thank you that you are here with us, you know us, and you love us.
Lord in your mercy....
All: Hear our prayer

Lord Jesus we thank you that you are with us in all we go through in this life, you know what it is to suffer, to grieve and to die. Your resurrection gives us hope that we too will one day be raised to new life in you.
Lord in your mercy.....
All: Hear our prayer

We pray for all those who suffer at this time, may they be comforted by your presence and know your strength and peace.
Lord in your mercy.....
All: Hear our prayer

We pray for all those who care for us here. Please fill them with your tender love and compassion and may they know your joy and peace in their work. Please bless them and their families.
Lord in your mercy.....
All: Hear our prayer

We pray for all our families, friends and loved ones both near and far. Please hold them in your loving care and bless them
Lord in your mercy.......
All: Hear our prayer

Meeting Jesus in a locked room

Welcome and Introduction

Opening Response:

Leader: Alleluia! Christ is risen!
All: **He is risen indeed**
                  Alleluia!

Jesus came and stood among them and said, "Peace be with you!"
(John 20: 19)

Hymn: Alleluia give thanks to the risen Lord

Confession:

Leader: Lord forgive us
All: **Lord forgive us and help us.**

Lord Jesus we come before you today just as we are with our strengths and weaknesses, our doubts and fears, our joys and sorrows.

For the times when we have closed ourselves to God and not loved him with all of our heart. Lord forgive us….

For the times when we have closed ourselves to one another and not loved one another fully. Lord forgive us…

May God our Father forgive us and help us to love him and our neighbours here that we might continue to grow together as a community of love and faith. **Amen**

Reading:	John 20:19-22, 24-29

Talk

The Peace:

Leader: Jesus said, "Peace be with you, as the Father has sent me, I am sending you." The peace of the Lord be always with you.

All: **And also with you**

Leader: Receive the Holy Spirit. Let us offer one another a sign of peace.

Hymn: Be still for the presence of the Lord

Prayers:

Leader: Lord in your mercy

All: **Hear our prayer**

Let us draw all these prayers together in the words of The Lord's Prayer

All: **Our Father who art in Heaven**

Hymn: Thine be the glory

Blessing

Leader: Peace be with you
Peace be within you
Peace to fill you
Peace to calm you
Peace to free you
Peace surround you
Peace to share with friend and stranger
The peace of God be with you always
Amen.

All: **The Grace**

Introduction to the service

I do hope that you all have had a very Happy Easter. Last time we were here was during Holy Week. We gave you all a palm cross and remembered Jesus riding into Jerusalem on a donkey with all the people singing Hosanna and hailing him as king. We also thought about his death on the cross on Good Friday. Now we are in this very special season of Easter, a joyful time, where we are thinking about Jesus alive, risen from the dead and spending time with his disciples. This period went on for about 6 weeks. Jesus' friends would gather together every day very much as we are today and he would often be there with them, helping them to understand the meaning of his death and

resurrection, preparing them to continue his mission in the world and forming them into the church. Whenever the early Christians met each other they would greet each other by saying "Christ is risen!" He is risen indeed Alleluia!" This is the Easter greeting that we are going to begin our service with…..

Talk

The reading we have just heard tells us the story of two occasions when Jesus appeared to his disciples. Both times they were gathered together and Jesus seems to have just walked through locked doors into the room. On the first Easter Sunday evening the friends were hiding. They were very afraid that following Jesus' crucifixion they would all be rounded up and killed as well. I imagine that they felt both afraid and directionless, after all, they had given up everything to follow Jesus – their homes and families. What was to become of them now?

In the midst of this turmoil, Jesus walks into the room and greets them, "Peace be with you, don't be afraid, it's really me, all is well, I'm alive again." I think they found it hard to believe that it was really him, it was a real shock after all they had been through to see him standing there before them. I think some of them thought they were seeing things. We know that one of the disciples Thomas was not there at the time and when they told him they had seen the Lord, he just couldn't believe it. We know the story…. A week later when Thomas is there this time, the same thing happens – Jesus walks into the room. Poor Thomas, what a shock! But I think we can identify with Thomas, can't we? Jesus asks us to believe in him even though we can't see him, and this is very difficult for some people – perhaps all of us at times.

The wonderful thing is that every time we gather together in this room to worship Jesus, the same thing happens again and again. Jesus walks into this room and says to us "Peace be with you." He knows all that we go through, and he says, "I'm here, it's really me, I'm alive, don't be afraid, believe."

In a moment I'm going to say the words of the peace and then come around and share the peace with you all. As I do this let's remember that even though we can't see him, Jesus is here with us and he gives us his peace.

Prayers

Lord Jesus we come before you today just as we are and ask that you would speak your peace into our hearts. Please calm our worries and fears and help us to feel secure in the knowledge that you hold us in the palm of your hand. Lord in your mercy…….Hear our prayer.

We pray for all those known to us who are suffering in any way in body mind or spirit, and especially for those in hospital. We pray that you would give them your peace and touch them with your healing and strength. Lord in your mercy…..

We pray that you would help us to reach out in love and peace to our friends and neighbours here. Lord in your mercy…..

We pray for all those who care for us here. Please bless them and their families and fill them with your tender care. Lord in your mercy….

We pray for all the troubled places in our world that there would be an end to hatred and fighting and that we would be able to live in peace with one another. Lord in your mercy……
The Lord's Prayer.

Meeting Jesus on the road to Emmaus

Picture: The road to Emmaus by the Benedictine Nuns of Turvey Abbey

Then their eyes were opened, and they recognised him… They asked each other, "Were not our hearts burning within us while he talked with us on the road and opened the scriptures to us?"(Luke 24:32)

Welcome and Introduction

Opening response:

Leader: Alleluia! Christ is risen!
**All: He is risen indeed
Alleluia!**

Hymn: Alleluia, alleluia, give thanks

Confession:
Leader: Lord forgive us
All: Lord forgive us and help us.

Lord Jesus we come before you today just as we are with our strengths and weaknesses, our doubts and fears, our joys and sorrows.

For the times when we have closed ourselves to God and not loved him with all of our heart. Lord forgive us….

For the times when we have closed ourselves to one another and not loved one another fully. Lord forgive us…

May God our Father forgive us and help us to love him and our neighbours that we might grow together as a community of love and faith. **Amen**

Dramatic Reading: Luke 24:13-35 and acting out the story

Talk

Hymn: Be still for the presence of the Lord

Prayers:
Leader: Lord in your mercy
All: **Hear our prayer**

Let us draw all these prayers together in the words of '
The Lord's Prayer

All: **Our Father in Heaven…..**

The Peace:

Leader: On the evening of the first day of the week,
when the disciples were together, Jesus
came and stood among them and said,
"Peace be with you."
The peace of the Lord be always with you.
All: **And also with you**

Leader: Let us offer one another a sign of peace

Hymn: Thank you Jesus

Blessing

Leader: God the Father,
by whose glory Christ was raised from the
dead strengthen us to walk with him in his
risen life and may God bless us, the Father,
the Son and the Holy Spirit. Amen.

All: **The Grace**

Luke 24:13-35 (NIV) On the Road to Emmaus

13 Now that same day two of the disciples were going to a village called Emmaus, about seven miles from Jerusalem. 14 They were talking with each other about everything that had happened. 15 As they talked and discussed these things with each other, Jesus himself came up and walked along with them; 16 but they were kept from recognizing him.

17 "What are you discussing together as you walk along?"

They stood still, their faces downcast. 18 One of them, named Cleopas, asked him, "Are you the only one visiting Jerusalem who does not know the things that have happened there in these days?"

19 "What things?"

"About Jesus of Nazareth. He was a prophet, powerful in word and deed before God and all the people. 20 The chief priests and our rulers handed him over to be sentenced to death, and they crucified him; 21 but we had hoped that he was the one who was going to redeem Israel. And what is more, it is the third day since all this took place"

22 In addition, some of our women amazed us. They went to the tomb early this morning 23 but didn't find his body. They came and told us that they had seen a vision of angels, who said he was alive. 24 Then some of our companions went to the tomb and found it just as the women had said, but they did not see Jesus."

25 "How foolish you are, and how slow to believe all that the prophets have spoken! 26 Did not the Messiah have to suffer these things and then enter his glory?"

27 And beginning with Moses and all the Prophets, he explained to them what was said in all the Scriptures concerning himself. 28 As they approached the village to which they were going, Jesus continued on as if he were going further. 29 But they urged him strongly,

"Stay with us, for it is nearly evening; the day is almost over." So he went in to stay with them. 30 When he was at the table with them, he took bread, gave thanks, broke it and began to give it to them. 31 Then their eyes were opened and they recognized him, "It's Jesus! It's Jesus!"

and he disappeared from their sight. 32 They asked each other,

"Were not our hearts burning within us while he talked with us on the road and opened the Scriptures to us?"

33 They got up and returned at once to Jerusalem. There they found the Eleven and those with them, assembled together 34 and saying, "It is true! The Lord has risen and has appeared to Simon." 35 Then the two told what had happened on the way, and how Jesus was recognized by them when he broke the bread.

"Jesus is alive! We met him on the road!"

Talk

We have read this lovely story of two Easter people. Two people who were clearly close friends of Jesus and his disciples. They had witnessed the terrible events in Jerusalem which had lead to Jesus' death on the cross. It is Sunday afternoon and they are walking home together, feeling shocked and bewildered, talking together and wondering what it all meant. They had pinned their hopes on Jesus, believing that he would be the one to liberate the Jews from the Romans. But now he was dead they must have felt very let down and disappointed. They have been left with that question Why? What did it all mean? Why had it all gone wrong? Why did Jesus have to die?

As they walked and talked and questioned, Jesus suddenly comes to join them. He listens to their questions and feelings and then he opens the scriptures to them to help them to understand who the Messiah really is and what he really came to do and why he had to die. These people do not realise it, but it is Jesus who is with them. They don't recognise that it is him walking along with them.

This story speaks to me so much about our own lives. Our lives can be a bit like that journey from Jerusalem to Emmaus. In a sense all of us are on our own journey through life making our way gradually to our eternal home. Life is full of ups and downs, joys and sorrows, births and deaths and at times we can go through suffering which leaves us asking those kinds of questions. Why did this happen to me? What does it mean? Where is God? In the church and here in our care home, I have a sense that we are journeying together with one another. We can share our burdens with each other and support and care for one another on the road. As we walk along together we may not realise it, but Jesus is walking along with us. He is there to lead and guide us, to comfort and help us. Like those disciples we are not alone on our journey through this life and particularly on this part of it in our care home. We have the support and care of one another here and even if like the disciples on the road to Emmaus we don't always recognise him, Jesus is here with us.

Let us be aware of the presence of Jesus here with us now as we sing our next hymn.

Be still for the presence of the Lord.

Prayers

As we come now to our time of prayer let us have a moments silence and be aware of the presence of Jesus with us now to lead and guide, to comfort and help, to cleanse and heal. Let us pray.

Silence

Lord Jesus we come before you now just as we are and ask that you will reveal yourself to us and minister to us your grace. Help us to be aware of your presence with us. Lord in your mercy....

Lord Jesus, we thank you that as we journey through this life you are always with us in everything we go through. We ask that you bless us, and give us your strength and comfort. Lord in your mercy.....

Lord Jesus we pray that you would help us to share your love with our brothers and sisters here in our care homes. Help us to support and care for one another as we journey together towards your Kingdom. Lord in your mercy.....

We pray for all those who care for us here in our care home. Please bless them and their families. May they be filled with your love and compassion and know your joy in their work. Lord in your mercy.....

We pray for all our families, friends and loved ones. Please bless them and be close to them. Lord in your mercy....

We pray for all those who are alone and who feel lonely and unloved, may they come to know that you are with them and you love them. Lord in your mercy.....

Let us draw all these prayers together in the words of
The Lord's Prayer

140

141

Meeting Jesus on the beach

Picture: Breakfast on the beach by the Benedictine Nuns
                                                      of Turvey Abbey

Welcome and Introduction

Opening Response:

Leader: Alleluia! Christ is risen!
All: **He is risen indeed**
                         Alleluia!

*Jesus said to them, "Come and have breakfast," None of the disciples dared to
ask him "who are you?" They knew it was the Lord.(John 21:12)*

Hymn: Praise my soul the king of Heaven

Confession:

Leader: Lord forgive us
All: **Lord forgive us and help us.**

Lord Jesus we come before you today just as we are with our
strengths and weaknesses, our doubts and fears, our joys and
sorrows.

For the times when we have closed ourselves to God and not
loved him with all our heart. Lord forgive us….

For the times when we have closed ourselves to one another
and not loved one another fully. Lord forgive us…

May God our Father forgive us and help us to love him and our
neighbours here that we might continue to grow together as a
community of love and faith. **Amen**

Reading: John 21: 1-14

Talk

Hymn: O Jesus I have promised

Prayers:
Leader: Lord in your mercy
All: **Hear our prayer**

Let us draw all these prayers together in the words of
The Lord's Prayer

All: **Our Father who art in Heaven**

Hymn: Thine be the glory

Blessing

Leader: God the Father,
                      by whose glory Christ was raised from the dead
                      strengthen us to walk with him in his risen life.
                      And may God bless us, keep us in his peace and
                      hold us in the palm of his hand. Amen.

All: **The Grace**

Talk

We are still in the Easter season and reading these wonderful stories of Jesus appearing to his disciples after his resurrection. This story is one of my favourites.

Have you ever thought about how the disciples felt after Jesus died on the cross? Not only had they witnessed the awfulness of his crucifixion, but now they were left alone with no leader, no direction. What were they supposed to do now? For three years they had followed Jesus. They had seen so many extraordinary things, had so many adventures and they thought they were going to share in his kingdom. But suddenly it was all finished. All over. Jesus was dead. The bottom had fallen out of their world. They simply did not know what to do next. And so, it was quite understandable when Peter suddenly announces that he is going fishing. Fishing was what he was doing when he first met Jesus. Fishing is what he knows how to do. His life with Jesus is finished, and so it makes sense to go back to his former life.

And so, what happens next? Well the other disciples decide to join him, and they go off fishing, but even though they are out all night, they don't catch a thing. I expect by morning Peter was really fed up. Not only has his life with Jesus come to an end, but now he seems to have forgotten how to catch fish as well. But as they are approaching the shore early in the morning they see a stranger standing there who asks them if they have caught anything and when they say "No", he tells them to throw their nets over the other side, and we know the rest of the story, they then haul in a huge catch of fish.

But what was really happening here?

I believe that Jesus was bringing the disciples right back to the beginning again. At the beginning of the story Jesus meets Peter and Andrew and James and John on the shore. The same thing happens. They have been fishing all night and caught nothing. On this occasion he tells them to push out into the deep for a catch and again they haul in a large catch. On this occasion he invites them to "Follow me and I will make you fishers of men." And so now, I believe that what Jesus was saying was, "Back then I called you away from your fishing profession to become fishers of men. I am still calling you to this mission. Don't go back to your former life as if you had never met me and heard my call. I am not dead, I am alive. This is not the end, it is only the beginning." And then he invites them to have breakfast with him on the beach. He gathers them together again as his disciples and in a sense re-calls them to their mission of following him, of living for him and reaching out to others in his name

It maybe that as you think back over your life, you may be able to remember special times when you were aware of Jesus calling to you to follow him. Today, as we gather together with Jesus a bit like those disciples on the beach. Jesus says to us, "Remember, that I have called you to follow me. Keep going, keep following me, keep living for me, keep reaching out in love to others. I am with you.

Our next hymn is a prayer to be able to keep following Jesus throughout the whole of life right to the end:

Oh Jesus, I have promised to serve thee to the end. O give me grace to follow my master and my friend

Prayers

Lord Jesus we thank you that whenever we meet together in this room you are with us just as you were with your disciples. May we be aware of your presence with us now.
Lord in your mercy………**hear our prayer.**

We thank you for the moments in our own lives when we have heard you calling to us, "Follow me." Please give us the courage and strength to keep following for the whole of our lives.
Lord in your mercy………**hear our prayer.**

We pray for all those who care for us here. For our managers that they may be guided by you in the running of the home. For our carers and volunteers that they may be filled with your compassion and gentleness. Please bless them and their families.
Lord in your mercy………**hear our prayer.**

We pray for all our families, friends and loved ones. Please be close to them and bless them wherever they are.
Lord in your mercy………**hear our prayer.**

We pray for all those known to us who are suffering in anyway in body, mind and spirit. Especially we pray for those in hospital at this time. Please be close to them and bring them your healing and peace.
Lord in your mercy………**hear our prayer.**

Ascension Day
Meeting Jesus on a mountain

Picture: The Ascension by The Benedictine Nuns
                                              of Turvey Abbey

Welcome and Introduction
Opening response

Leader: Alleluia! Christ is risen!
All: **He is risen indeed**
                  Alleluia!

Hymn: Crown him with many crowns

Confession

Leader: Lord forgive us
All: **Lord forgive us and help us.**

Lord Jesus we come before you today just as we are with our
strengths and weaknesses, our doubts and fears, our joys and
sorrows.

For the times when we have closed ourselves to God and not
loved him with all of our heart. Lord forgive us….

For the times when we have closed ourselves to one another
and not loved one another fully. Lord forgive us…

May God our Father forgive us and help us to love him and our
neighbours here, that we might continue to grow together as a
community of love and faith. **Amen**

Dramatic Reading: Acts 1:1-11

Talk

Hymn: **Spirit of the living God**
                    Fall afresh on me
                    Break me, melt me
                    Mould me, fill me.
                    Spirit of the living God
                    Fall afresh on me.

Prayers:
Leader: Lord send your spirit…..
All: **Come Holy Spirit**

Let us draw all these prayers together in the words of
The Lord's Prayer

All: **Our Father who art in Heaven……**

Hymn: Alleluia Sing to Jesus

Blessing:

                    May the Love of the Spirit
                    Enfold you
                    May the strength of the Spirit
                    Uphold you
                    May the Peace of the Spirit
                    Refresh you
                    May the joy of the Spirit
                    Uplift you
                    May the Light of the Spirit
                    Shine on you
                    May the Mercy of the Spirit
                    Rekindle you
                    May the Spirit renew your innermost being.

All: **The Grace**

Introduction to the service

Today is a special day when we celebrate the Ascension of Jesus. It ends the Easter season. Since Easter Day we have been celebrating the Resurrection and telling the stories of Jesus' appearances to his disciples over a period of 40 days. He kept showing them that he was indeed alive and talking with him. And then one day he gathers a large group of them and takes them up to the top of a mountain where they see him rise into the sky and then above the clouds and gone.

Here in this picture we can see the disciples looking up into the sky as he disappears and the outline here of the two angels the disciples saw who tell them that Jesus will one day come again. As Jesus ascends to Heaven, he leaves the disciples with one last instruction: Stay in Jerusalem and wait for my gift – the gift of the Holy Spirit.

Dramatic Reading Acts 1:1-11 (NIV)

Jesus taken up into Heaven

1 In my former book, Theophilus, I wrote about all that Jesus began to do and to teach 2 until the day he was taken up to heaven, after giving instructions through the Holy Spirit to the apostles he had chosen. 3 After his suffering, he presented himself to them and gave many convincing proofs that he was alive. He appeared to them over a period of forty days and spoke about the kingdom of God. 4 On one occasion, while he was eating with them, he gave them this command:

"Do not leave Jerusalem, but wait for the gift my Father promised, which you have heard me speak about. 5 For John baptized with water, but in a few days you will be baptized with the Holy Spirit."

6 Then they gathered around him and asked him,

"Lord, are you at this time going to restore the kingdom to Israel?"

7 "It is not for you to know the times or dates the Father has set by his own authority. 8 But you will receive power when the Holy Spirit comes on you; and you will be my witnesses in Jerusalem, and in all Judea and Samaria, and to the ends of the earth."

9 After he said this, he was taken up before their very eyes, and a cloud hid him from their sight.

10 They were looking intently up into the sky as he was going, when suddenly two men dressed in white stood beside them.

11 "Men of Galilee," they said, "why do you stand here looking into the sky? This same Jesus, who has been taken from you into heaven, will come back in the same way you have seen him go into heaven."

Talk

We are now at the end of the Easter season. The disciples and friends of Jesus have been together in Jerusalem for a period of 40 days from the time of his Resurrection. And during that time Jesus has appeared to them many times. In our services we have remembered the time when Jesus meets Mary Magdalen in the garden. When he meets two disciples who are on their way home to Emmaus and another time when Jesus walked into the room and said to them 'Peace be with you.' Last week we remembered when Jesus met his disciples on the beach at Lake Galilee and invited them to come and have breakfast. It must have been a very special time for the disciples, seeing Jesus risen from the dead, listening to his teaching and feeling close to him. But also, they were hearing about the mission that Jesus was giving them to carry on his life and his work on earth.

Today we celebrate Ascension Day, the day when Jesus' ministry here on earth came to its completion. The gospels tell us that Jesus and his disciples go up to the top of a high mountain and there he blesses them. As they watch he is lifted into the sky, into the clouds and is gone. I think if I had been there that I might have felt rather bereft to see him leave like that. But in the gospel Jesus has prepared his friends for this moment. He tells them that he must go back to be with his Father in Heaven, but also, he tells them that he is going to prepare a place there for all of them and all of us. We know that even now Jesus is making ready our places in Heaven so that we can go there and be with him forever. Also, Jesus made a promise that he would never leave us nor forsake us. But how could this be if the disciples watched him leave them? Well, they were to wait for the Holy Spirit- the spirit of Jesus who would come to them. In this mysterious, invisible way Jesus would be with them, inside them, all around them. He would be with them all the time wherever they were.

The same is true for all of us here. Jesus is with us in the person of the Holy Spirit. In a couple of weeks, we will remember the time when the Holy Spirit was poured out on the disciples in a special way at Pentecost and so like them we too are waiting for the spirit to come to refresh us, to strengthen us, to help us everyday to live for Jesus. So as this Easter season comes to a close, we now enter into a new season – the season of the Spirit. Let us, like them open our hearts and hands to welcome the Holy Spirit as we sing the next hymn which is on your order of service.

Spirit of the living God

Prayers

Lord send your Spirit.....
Come Holy Spirit....

As we are gathered together like the early disciples waiting for the coming of the Holy Spirit we thank you Lord for your promise to us that you would never leave us nor forsake us. Lord send your spirit, **Come Holy Spirit.**

Lord Jesus we pray that we might always feel your presence near to us here, especially when we feel lonely, cut off from family and friends and far from home. Lord send your Spirit...

We pray for all those who care for us here, for the staff and volunteers and for our families and friends who visit us. Please bless them, fill them with your tender love and compassion.
Lord send your Spirit...

We pray for all those known to us who are suffering in any way in body, mind or spirit. We especially pray for those in hospital. May they be aware of your loving presence with them to heal and strengthen. Lord send your Spirit....

We pray that your spirit may be poured out in our world to bring peace and an end to the suffering of so many because of war, famine and natural disaster. Lord send your Spirit......

Let us draw all these prayers together in the words of **the Lord's Prayer.**

PENTECOST

Celebrating the Season of Pentecost

Introduction

.At our Ascension Day service we re-enacted the last of Jesus' meetings with his disciples after his resurrection. With the disciples we stand on the mountain and watch him ascend into the clouds as he returns to his Father. We are left with Jesus'' instruction - 'Wait for my gift of the Holy Spirit.' So it is with a sense of great anticipation that we come to our celebration of Pentecost. We want to create an atmosphere of joy and praise. Some residents may enjoy playing a tambourine. Often we use the simple songs of the spirit suggested in the following pages.

We use a very simple prayer, 'Come Holy Spirit.' We remind ourselves of the wonderful fact that we are never alone, but that Jesus is always with us in the person of the Holy Spirit. He is the Living Water that flows into our souls renewing and reviving us when we feel weak or sad or tired.

Spirit of the Living God
Fall afresh on me
Melt me, mould me, fill me, use me
Spirit of the Living God
Fall afresh on me

Planning Pentecost Services

Mood and atmosphere:	Joy and praise
Colours:	Red
Visual display:	Symbols of the Holy Spirit - dove, candle (fire), water, jug
Theme, Story, Message:	The story of the coming of the Holy Spirit at Pentecost
	Jesus made present to us now in the person of the Spirit
	Living water
Bible Readings:	Acts 2, John 14, 16
	John 4: 4-15
Hymns:	Breathe on me breath of God
	Walk in the light
	Spirit of God (Skye boat song melody)
	Spirit of the Living God
	Peace is flowing like a river
	When the Spirit of the Lord
	Shine Jesus shine
	Father we adore you
	Let your living water, flow over my soul
Prayers:	Come Holy Spirit
Visual aids:	Model of hands open
	Encourage people to open their hands as if receiving a gift and to pray 'Come Holy Spirit'
	Tambourines and bells to play while singing songs of praise.

Pentecost
Season of the Spirit

Visual display:	Symbols of the Spirit – candle (fire), Picture of a dove

Welcome and Introduction

Come Holy Spirit, fill the hearts of your faithful people, and kindle in us the fire of your love; through Jesus Christ our Lord. Amen

Opening response:

Leader:	The Lord is here
All:	**His Spirit is with us**
Hymn:	Spirit of God - (Skye boat song melody)

Confession

Leader:	Lord forgive us
All:	**Lord forgive us and help us.**

Lord Jesus we come before you today just as we are with our strengths and weaknesses, our doubts and fears, our joys and sorrows.

For the times when we have closed ourselves to God and not loved him with all our heart. Lord forgive us....

For the times when we have closed ourselves to one another and not loved one another fully. Lord forgive us...

May God our Father forgive us and help us to love him and our neighbours here, that we might continue to grow together as a community of love and faith **Amen.**

Reading:	Acts 2 :1-12

Talk

Hymn:	Spirit of the Living God

The Peace:
Leader: Jesus came and stood among them and said, "Peace be with you, as the Father has sent me, so I am sending you." And with that he breathed on them and said, "Receive the Holy Spirit."

The peace of the Lord be always with you

All: **And also with you**

Chaplains offer the peace saying, "Peace be with you. Receive the Holy Spirit."

Prayers:
Leader: Lord we pray to you
All: **Come Holy Spirit**

Let us draw all these prayers together in the words of
The Lord's Prayer

All: **Our Father who art in Heaven……**

Hymn: Walk in the Light

Blessing: May the Holy Spirit renew us
And strengthen our hearts in his love

May the Spirit shine on us
And illumine our paths in life

May the Holy Spirit rest on us
And keep us from all harm

May the Holy Spirit bless us
Now and for ever
Amen

All: **The Grace**

Talk

Today we are thinking about the coming of the Holy Spirit on the day of Pentecost.

Before Jesus had ascended into Heaven he had told his disciples to stay in Jerusalem and to wait for the gift of the Holy Spirit. And so everyday we know they gathered together in a room a bit like this one to pray and to wait for the coming of the Spirit. On the day of Pentecost, we know there were about 120 of them in the room including the women and Jesus' mother Mary.

When the Spirit came something rather mysterious happened. They described it like a violent wind and they saw what looked like fire above each person's head and they all found that they were able to praise God in other languages.

This was the gift that Jesus had promised. From then on, the followers of Jesus would never be alone. They would have the Spirit of Jesus living in their hearts. He would always be with them as an inner presence. Jesus tells us that the Spirit has been sent to guide us, to show us the truth, to bring us peace, to help us to live together in unity. He comes as one of our hymns says, to cleanse and heal, to minister his grace. The spirit has been given so that we might have the strength to love God with all our hearts and our neighbours as ourselves.

Today I have brought this special candle holder which shows hands open as if to receive a gift. Can I ask you all to hold your hands open like this. It is a sign that we are ready to receive the gift of the spirit. As we sing and then in the silence that follows you may like to quietly pray your own prayer asking for the Holy Spirit to come and give you his strength and peace or anything else that you feel you need at this time.
Come Holy Spirit

Song: Spirit of the Living God

Silence

Prayers

We come now to our time of prayer. Let us hold our hands open to receive the gift of the Holy Spirit. After each prayer I will say Lord we pray to you and you respond
Come Holy Spirit.

Lord Jesus as we gather together in this upper room like the early disciples, we too wait for the gift of the Holy Spirit. Lord we pray to you.
Come Holy Spirit.

We pray that you would give us the strength and help we need to live lives of love and service to God and our neighbours here. Lord we pray to you.
Come Holy Spirit.

We pray for all those who care for us here, for staff and volunteers, for families and friends. May they be blessed and filled with your love and compassion. Lord we pray to you.
Come Holy Spirit.

We pray for all those known to us who are suffering in anyway in body, mind or spirit. We remember those in hospital at this time. May they know your healing and strength. Lord we pray to you.
Come Holy Spirit.

Let us draw all these prayers together in the words of **The Lord's Prayer.**

Woman at the well
Season of the Spirit

Picture: The woman at the well by The Benedictine
          Nuns of Turvey Abbey

Welcome and Introduction

Come Holy Spirit, fill the hearts of your faithful people, and kindle in us the fire of your love; through Jesus Christ our Lord. Amen

Opening response:
Leader: The Lord is here
All: **His Spirit is with us**

Hymn: The Spirit comes to set us free

Confession
Leader: Lord forgive us
All: **Lord forgive us and help us.**

Lord Jesus we come before you today just as we are with our strengths and weaknesses, our doubts and fears, our joys and sorrows.

For the times when we have closed ourselves to God and not loved him with all of our heart. Lord forgive us….

For the times when we have closed ourselves to one another and not loved one another fully. Lord forgive us…

May God our Father forgive us and help us to love him and our neighbours here, that we might continue to grow together as a community of love and faith. **Amen**

Reading: John 4:4-15

Talk

Hymn: Peace is flowing like a river

Prayers:
Leader: Lord we pray to you
All: **Come Holy Spirit**

Let us draw all these prayers together in the words of
The Lord's Prayer

All: **Our Father who art in Heaven……**

Hymn: Spirit of God (Skye boat song melody)

Blessing: May the Holy Spirit renew us
                And strengthen our hearts in his love

                May the Spirit shine on us
                And illumine our paths in life

                May the Holy Spirit rest on us
                And keep us from all harm

                May the Holy Spirit bless us
                Now and for ever
                Amen

All: **The Grace**

Talk

Last week in our service we celebrated the coming of the Holy Spirit at Pentecost. We remembered that Jesus' last instruction to the disciples when he said goodbye to them was wait in Jerusalem for the gift of the Holy Spirit. And this is what the disciples did. They waited and then on the day of Pentecost they were all gathered together and there was the sound of a great wind in the room and they saw tongues of fire which rested on their heads and they found they could speak in other languages.

In today's reading we listen in to a conversation between Jesus and a Samaritan woman who has come to be known as the Woman at the Well. They are talking about water. Jesus doesn't refer to the Holy Spirit, but he tells the woman about a gift he would like to give her which is a special kind of water. He tells her that the Holy Spirit is like an ever-flowing spring of water and that if she drinks of this water she will never be thirsty again. It was difficult for the woman to understand what Jesus meant. All she knew was that she had to keep coming every day to draw water because every day her water ran out. But Jesus knew that there was more to it than that. He knew that inside herself she felt empty and thirsty and was longing to be loved. Jesus was saying to this woman that if she would open her heart she could receive the Holy Spirit which is like a special kind of water that would fill her and meet a deep need in her so that she would never be thirsty again and she says, "Sir, please give me this water."

Last week I encouraged all of us to open our hands to receive a gift like the hands in this candle holder and to pray a very simple prayer that I myself often pray which simply goes; 'Come Holy Spirit.' Jesus tells us in this story that the Holy Spirit is like an ever flowing stream and that whenever we feel dry or thirsty or empty, whenever we feel weak or alone or sad we can come and be filled again. The Holy Spirit is a gift which is always there for us.

But how do we receive this gift of the Holy Spirit? It is very simple. In a quiet moment we can just open our hands and our hearts and pray that simple prayer 'Come Holy Spirit' and ask for whatever we need. I'm struggling Lord, Come Holy Spirit fill me with your strength. I feel lonely Lord, Come Holy Spirit and fill me with your love. I feel unwell today, Lord, Come Holy Spirit and restore me to health. I feel down today Lord; Come Holy Spirit lift me up and give me your joy.

Our next song is all about the Holy Spirit like a river filling us with peace, love and joy

Peace is flowing like a river

Prayers:

Lord we pray to you
Come Holy Spirit.

Lord Jesus we thank you for your invitation to receive the gift of your Holy Spirit. Help us now to open our hands and our hearts to receive you. Lord we pray to you. **Come Holy Spirit.**

We pray for ourselves as we go through the ups and downs of life. We ask that the gift of your Holy Spirit would bring us peace, love and joy in our life together and the strength to truly love one another. Please lift us up when we feel down and come close to us when we feel alone. Lord we pray to you.....

We pray for all those known to us who are suffering in any way in body, mind or spirit. Especially we pray for those in hospital. Please come with your strength and healing with your comfort and hope. Lord we pray to you.....

We pray for all those who care for us a here. For our managers that they would receive your wisdom and guidance. For the staff and volunteers that they would be filled with your gifts of love, patience and compassion. Lord we pray to you....

Let us draw all these prayers together in the words of
The Lord's Prayer.

HARVEST

Celebrating the Season of Harvest

Introduction

.Harvest is a wonderful season to celebrate in care homes. It coincides with late summer/autumn and does not have to be a one off event but can be enjoyed throughout the end of September and into October. It is colourful and sensory. It stimulates memories of Harvest festivals celebrated at school or Sunday School and in church. Residents all know the traditional Harvest hymns and can be involved in setting up displays of flowers and food.

Some care homes will collect food items to be donated to a local food bank. We like to invite a representative from the food bank to come to our Harvest festival to speak about their work and to receive the food that has been collected by the staff and relatives of the home. This helps the home to feel that they are giving something to their local community.

In this section of the book we offer a variety of services for this season which explore themes of thanksgiving for God's provision, giving to those who are disadvantaged, the generosity of God and meeting God in his creation.

There are examples of visual displays and activities we have enjoyed doing with our residents such as flower arranging, autumn collages, bulb planting, bread baking and flower pot men.

We also like to go out for walks with our residents into the garden or to nearby parks to enjoy the changing colours of the season and bring back items we can use for our Harvest displays and collages.

Planning Harvest Services

Mood and atmosphere: Thanksgiving

Colours: Autumn colours - gold, orange, brown

Visual display: Picture: The Sower

Flowers, fruits and vegetables

Harvest gifts - tins and packets

Theme, Story, Message: Thanksgiving for the Harvest and for all God's provision

Thanksgiving for the Harvest of our lives

Prayers for those who are disadvantaged

Meeting God in his creation

Bible Readings: See the readings suggested

Hymns: We plough the fields and scatter

Come ye thankful

For the fruits of all creation

Now thank we all our God

Thank you Lord for this fine day

When I needed a neighbour

All creatures of our God and king

All things bright and beautiful

For the beauty of the earth

Prayers: Prayers of thanksgiving

Visual aids and 3D Activities: Flower arranging

Seed and bulb planting

Bread baking - wheat sheaf loaf

Apple pie making

Harvest crafts - leaf collages

Harvest
Gifts

Harvest
Food Bank Service

Visual display: Harvest gifts, wheat sheaf loaf,
arrangements of flowers and fruit.

Welcome and Introduction

Opening Poem- by Susan Wagstaff

All things bright and beautiful
All creatures great and small
We gather here at Harvest time
To celebrate them all

We watch the nights start drawing in
And feel the autumn breeze
As branches sway from side to side
They drop their golden leaves

We plough our fields and scatter Lord
The good seed on the land
And watch it grow from seed to plants
Protected by your loving hand

We've filled a box with lots of food
And know that when our box is gone
Each item bought and given with love
For people who have none

Hymn: Come ye thankful people

Let us confess our sin:

Leader: Lord forgive us
All: **Lord forgive us and help us.**

For the times we have forgotten to love you and give you thanks for all your goodness. Lord forgive us....

For the times we have been unkind or forgotten to love those around us.
Lord forgive us.....

Lord forgive us and help us to love you and our neighbours that we might grow together as a community of love and faith.

Reading:	Matthew 25: 34 – 40
Talk:	From a representative of a local Food bank
Hymn:	When I needed a neighbour
Prayers Leader:	Lord in your mercy
All:	**Hear our prayer**

Let us draw all these prayers together in the words of
The Lord's Prayer

All:	**Our Father who art in Heaven......**
Hymn:	We plough the fields
Blessing:	**Psalm 67** May God be gracious to us and bless us And make his face to shine upon us May the peoples praise you, O God May all the peoples praise you Then the land will yield its harvest And God our God will bless us.

May God bless us and keep us and all those for whom we have prayed today. And may he hold us in the palm of his hand.
Amen

All:	**The Grace**

Talk

Invite a representative from a local Food bank to come to the service and speak about their work. Ask them to bring photos and examples of a typical bag of food that they would give to a needy family.

Ask several residents to present a box of basket of harvest gifts that have been donated by relatives and staff to the representative to take to the Food bank.

Harvest Prayers (in large print)
For residents to pray during a Harvest Festival Service

Dear Lord,

We thank you for this beautiful season of Harvest and for the abundance of fruit and vegetables, wheat and grain. We thank you for the farmers and for all those who work in food production so that we can have food on our tables. We pray for people in our country and in the world, who do not have enough to eat and ask you to bless those who are helping them.

Lord in your mercy….. **hear our prayer.**

Dear Lord,

We thank you for providing everything we need. Thank you for our home, thank you that we are warm and safe and comfortable. We pray for people in our country and in the world, who are homeless and poor, and we ask you to bless the work of all those who are helping them.

Lord in your mercy…..**hear our prayer.**

Dear Lord,

We thank you for all those who care for us, for our families and friends who come to visit us and for the carers and volunteers. Please bless all those who look after us. We pray for all those in our country and in the world, who have no one to care for them, those who feel lonely and lost. Please be close to them and let them know that you love them.

Lord in your mercy…..**hear our prayer.**

Harvest Festival

Welcome and Introduction

Opening Poem- by Susan Wagstaff

All things bright and beautiful
All creatures great and small
We gather here at Harvest time
To celebrate them all

We watch the nights start drawing in
And feel the autumn breeze
As branches sway from side to side
They drop their golden leaves

We plough our fields and scatter Lord
The good seed on the land
And watch it grow from seed to plants
Protected by your loving hand

We've filled a box with lots of food
And know that when our box is gone
Each item bought and given with love
For people who have none

Hymn: For the fruits of all creation (Tune- All through the night)

Let us confess our sin

Leader: Lord forgive us
All: **Lord forgive us and help us.**

For the times we have forgotten to love you and give you
thanks for all your goodness. Lord forgive us….

For the times we have been unkind or forgotten to love those around us. Lord forgive us…..

Lord forgive us and help us to love you and our neighbours that we might grow together as a community of love and faith.

Reading: Psalm 95: 1-6

Talk:

Hymn: All things bright and beautiful

Prayers
Leader: Lord we give you thanks
All: **Thank you Lord**

Let us draw all these prayers together in the words of **The Lord's Prayer**

All: **Our Father who art in Heaven……**

Hymn: We plough the fields

Blessing: **Psalm 67**
                  May God be gracious to us and bless us
                  And make his face to shine upon us
                  May the peoples praise you, O God
                  May all the peoples praise you
                  Then the land will yield its harvest
                  And God our God will bless us.

                  May God bless us and keep us and all those
                  for whom we have prayed today. And may he
                  hold us in the palm of his hand. **Amen**

All: **The Grace**

Talk

Harvest Festival is traditionally a time to say a special thank you to God for all his provision. For taking care of our needs, providing us with a roof over our heads and food on the table. This psalm talks about God being our God and that we are his people the sheep of his pasture. We can imagine ourselves like little sheep being looked after by the Good Shepherd.

It is so easy for us to not notice all that God gives us or to take it for granted. But if we open our ears, our eyes and are hearts we will be able to see and hear and receive his gifts to us. I have been thinking about some of the things that we might want to give thanks for here.

I know that some of you get a lot of pleasure looking out of your bedroom windows or the lounge windows at the garden. There is a beautiful apple tree and other shrubs which are just coming into their autumn glory.

Many of you tell me how caring the staff are here, how kind, helpful and friendly they are and that you receive such loving care from them. Some of you have made some good friends here with other residents and the staff. We give thanks for friendship and for all the love shared with one another.

Many of you tell me that you enjoy the activities that go on here. Some of you join in with the day care activities and lots of you with the activities that the Gift of Years do. Often the home is full of flowers when you have all been flower arranging. And we give thanks for the great gift of music which lifts our spirits and brings us joy.

Then there are the simple things of life that perhaps all of us do take for granted – a warm safe place to live, good food on the table, a warm bed to sleep in, people who love us.

As we sing our next hymn let us think of all the things we would like to say thank you to God for.

Hymn All things bright and beautiful

Prayers

At this Harvest time let us open our eyes, our ears and our hearts to notice and give thanks for all God gives to us everyday. Let us pray…

Heavenly Father we thank you so much for all your gifts to us here. We thank you for the comfort and security of this home, for the beauty of the garden and that we have everything we need. Lord we give you thanks…..

We thank you for our wonderful staff and volunteers who care for us and for all our families and friends who visit us and for members of the churches who come to minister to us. Lord we give you thanks….

We thank you for loving us so much and for being with us every day and in everything we go through. Lord we give you thanks….

At this harvest time, we think of all those in our world who don't have a warm, safe place to live, for those who don't have enough to eat, for those who do not know the love and care of family and friends. We pray for an end to conflict and injustice and pray for a fairer world where we may live together in peace.

The Lord's Prayer

Seasonal Harvest Service

Welcome and Introduction

Opening response:

Leader:	Let this day be full of your beauty and brightness
All:	**Lord hear us**

Leader:	That we may know your presence and your peace
All:	**Lord hear us**

Leader:	That we may experience your grace and glory
All:	**Lord hear us**

Leader:	That we may be one with you and your creation
All:	**Lord hear us**

Leader:	That we may be aware of you in and through and above all things
All:	**Lord hear us**

Hymn: All things bright and beautiful

Let us confess our sin:

Leader:	Lord forgive us
All:	**Lord forgive us and help us.**

For the times we have forgotten to love you and give you thanks
for all your goodness. Lord forgive us....

For the times we have been unkind or forgotten to love those around us. Lord forgive us.....

Lord forgive us and help us to love you and our neighbours that we might grow together as a community of love and faith.

Reading: Eccl 3:1-11

Talk

Hymn: We plough the fields and scatter

Prayers
Leader: Lord in your mercy
All: **Hear our prayer**

Let us draw all these prayers together in the words of
The Lord's Prayer

All: **Our Father who art in Heaven……**

Hymn: Great is thy faithfulness

Blessing: God has made everything beautiful in his time.
                         He has set eternity in our hearts.

                         May God bless us and hold each one of us in
                         the palm of his hand. **Amen**

All: **The Grace**

Introduction to the service

Last time we were here together we were celebrating Harvest Festival. Harvest is a lovely time of year to remember to say thank you to God for all his provision. Today we are going to continue with the harvest theme. But instead of thinking about the harvest of food, in this service we are going to say thank you to God for the Harvest of our lives......

Seasonal Harvest Talk

One of the things I really love is the changing seasons and I do especially love this autumn time of year when the colours of the leaves are so beautiful and there are berries and apples, plums pears.
There is something of a rhythm to our lives – we know what to expect.

This reading from the book of Ecclesiastes is all about the changing season of our lives......

Reading

The writer of Ecclesiastes is describing how life is. He speaks of how there is a time to be born and a time to die, there are good times and bad times, times to laugh and dance and times to weep and mourn. There are busy times and slower times, active times and waiting times. We can all relate to this passage of scripture because it is our human experience.

Harvest is a time when the crops of cereals, fruits and vegetables are all ripe and ready to gather in before the winter frost comes. It is an opportunity to notice all that God has given us, all his provision for us and to give thanks. But also, Harvest is a time when we can look back over the seasons of our lives and give thanks for all our fruitfulness. We can give thanks for our families and friends, for our homes and material possessions, for our work, for all the activities we have enjoyed, for all our gifts and abilities, for God's protection over us, for good health and well-being for the strength to overcome the hardships and difficulties. It is good to take time to look back and give thanks. All these things are gifts from God.

So, when you have some quiet moments you might like to just have a think back over the seasons of your life and give thanks to God for his provision and for all your fruitfulness.

Let's give thanks in the words of the next hymn.

We plough the fields...

Prayers

As we come now to our time of prayer, let us have a moment of silence to think back over the seasons of our lives and give thanks to God for all his gifts.

As we look back over our lives, we thank you for our childhoods and growing up years, our working lives, our home-making, for holidays, hobbies and pastimes, for all that we have given and received from our neighbours, our communities and church families. We give thanks for everything which has made life meaningful. We thank you for all the gifts and abilities which we have used well to bring joy to ourselves and others. Lord in your mercy.....

We thank you God for your constant faithfulness to us throughout all the seasons of our lives for your strength and protection and promise to bring us home. Lord in your mercy.....

We thank you for our families and friends, for all those who have been close to us over the years and who have shared our lives. We thank you for our community here, for the care of the staff and volunteers and all the love and friendship which we share with one another. Lord in your mercy.....

Let us draw all these prayers together in the words of **the Lord's Prayer**....

AUTUMNAL
LEAF COLLAGES

Meeting God in His Creation

Visual
display: Examples of resident's artwork and handicrafts

Welcome and introduction

Opening response:

Leader: Let this day be full of your beauty and brightness
All: **Lord hear us**

Leader: That we may know your presence and your peace
All: **Lord hear us**

Leader: That we may experience your grace and glory
All: **Lord hear us**

Leader: That we may be one with you and your creation
All: **Lord hear us**

Leader: That we may be aware of you in and through and
                above all things
All: **Lord hear us**

Hymn: All creatures of our God and king

Confession

Leader: Lord forgive us
              Lord forgive us and help us.

For the times we have forgotten to love you and give you thanks for all your goodness. Lord forgive us….

For the times we have been unkind or forgotten to love those around us. Lord forgive us…..

179

Lord forgive us and help us to love you and our neighbours that we might grow together as a community of love and faith.

Reading: Psalm 8: 1-9

Talk with creation pictures on Power Point

Hymn: For the beauty of the Earth
Prayers
Leader: Lord in your mercy
All: **Hear our prayer**

Let us draw all these prayers together in the words of
The Lord's Prayer

All: **Our Father who art in Heaven......**

Hymn: Oh Lord my God

Blessing:
          Lord, help us this day
          To look into the depths
          And see with the heart
          To behold the miracle of life
          To rejoice in the mystery of growth
          To bow before the otherness of creation
          To love the uniqueness of everything
          To accept the strangeness of all
          Give us, Lord, the joy of seeing
          Of looking with the eyes of the heart

          May God bless us and hold each one of us in the
          palm of his hand.

All: **The Grace**

YouTube: Wonderful World by Louis Armstrong video by Gabrielle Marie

Introduction to the service

We are still in the Harvest season of the year and right in the middle of autumn. I always really enjoy my journey here at this time of year. I love to see the colours of the trees in all their autumn glory. Today I want us to think about how we meet God and experience God in his creation.

Talk

Many of you may not know this, but we have some wonderful artists living here and I have been able to borrow some of their art work to show you. You can tell a lot about artists just from looking at their art work, I think.

Here is something that E made – it's called decoupage.
It involves cutting out tiny pieces of paper very carefully with a knife or scissors and sticking them together to build up a picture. I understand it takes a long time. E must be a very patient person with an eye for detail.

Here is something that B made – it's a beautiful wall hanging with pictures of the nativity. I will be putting it up in here later on for Christmas. It's been made very carefully, with tiny stitches to make the quilting. B is a rather quiet lady who doesn't blow her own trumpet, but she is always thinking of others and likes to make things for other people that they will find useful. I was thrilled when she made this for me to use.

We also have our very own florist – C our expert flower arranger. Here she is with her Harvest creation. C has a real eye for how colour and shape go together. This is the beautiful cross of flowers she made on Good Friday last year. She is often creating arrangements that make our home look beautiful and that we can all enjoy looking at.

And we have our very own P who is a gifted musician and likes to use his art to create a happy atmosphere, to make us laugh, to bring us joy and lift our spirits.

So just by looking at all this art work we can know something about the artist.

It is a little bit like this with God too. It can be hard to know God – he is a rather mysterious character and we are usually not able to know him with our senses – so we can't see him or hear him or touch him. But one of the ways we can come to know him is by looking at his creation, which is his art work.

Picture of a sunset
I have a few pictures here of God's creation which give us some idea of what God might be like. We see that God likes to stun us with his beauty. Did you ever see a beautiful sunset and sense God's presence in the stillness of the evening?

Picture of mountains
Whenever I see mountains it makes me think that God must be very great and majestic. I wonder did you ever see some grandiose scenery on holiday and find yourself exclaiming wow!! That's amazing.

Picture of a baby
Some people are very aware of God's presence at the birth of their children. Lots of new parents have a sense that creating a new life has happened with the help of God. Seeing this picture of this new born baby reminds us that God is close to all of us who are weak and vulnerable. He loves all his little ones.

Pictures of an emu and anteater
I think that when we look at some of God's creatures, we have to agree that he must have a sense of humour!

Pictures of parrots, Zebras and people of different nationalities
God is rather extravagant and likes variety. Eg. Parrots are very bright and colourful, and Zebras are black and white. It wouldn't do for us all to be the same. (People of different nationalities.) God really likes to have a big variety of people who make up his family.

At the end of the service we are going to watch a little film of God's creation and as you watch it you might want to give thanks for our wonderful world. God is reaching out to us, revealing himself to us through his creation. In a quiet moment you might want to think back and remember any times when you were especially aware of God's presence with you.

Hymn   For the beauty
             A hymn of thanksgiving for creation

Prayers
As we come now to our time of prayer, let us give thanks that God gives himself to us in the beauty and wonder of his creation.

Heavenly father, we thank you for the beauty of this autumn season, for the vibrant colours and for the harvest of fruits and berries. We thank you for the mown grass turned into hay by the sun for the animals during the winter and the ploughed fields, empty and resting in preparation for new growth in the spring. Lord in your mercy.....

We thank you for all the moments in our lives when we have been especially aware of your presence in creation. Lord in your mercy.....

We pray for all those who care for us here, for the staff and volunteers and for our families and friends who visit us. Please bless them and help them to be aware of you in the care that they give and the love that they share. Lord in your mercy....

We pray for all those who are suffering in our world in anyway. Especially we pray for all those who have no one to pray for them, no one to love them. May they experience your tender love and the love of your people. Lord in your mercy....

The Lord's Prayer

The Vine and the Branches

Visual display: Vine leaves and grapes

Welcome and Introduction

Opening Response

Leader:	Let this day be Full of your beauty and brightness
All:	**Lord, hear us**
Leader:	That we may know Your presence and your peace
All:	**Lord, hear us**
Leader:	That we may experience Your grace and your glory
All:	**Lord, hear us**
Leader:	That we may be one With you and creation
All:	**Lord, hear us**
Leader:	That we may be aware of you In and through and above all things
All:	**Lord, hear us**
Hymn:	All people that on Earth

Let us confess our sin:

Leader: Lord forgive us
    Lord forgive us and help us.

For the times we have forgotten to love you and give you
thanks for all your goodness. Lord forgive us….

For the times we have been unkind or forgotten to love those around us.
Lord forgive us…..

Lord forgive us and help us to love you and our neighbours that we might grow together as a community of love and faith.

Reading: John 15: 1-8

Talk

Hymn: In heavenly love abiding

Prayers
Leader: Lord in your mercy
All: **Hear our prayer**

Let us draw all these prayers together in the words of
The Lord's Prayer

All: **Our Father who art in Heaven……**

Hymn: O love that will not let me go.

Blessing: As the Father has loved me, so have I loved you.
                 Now remain in my love and be filled with my joy.
                 You are my friends. May God bless us and keep
                 us and hold us in the palm of his hand. **Amen**

All: **The Grace**

Talk

I was inspired to choose this reading for us today, by my garden. It was a bit of a shock to come home after 2 weeks away on holiday to find that it had gone wild and overgrown especially the vine. We have a grapevine which grew from a seed that my husband happened to drop by the back door. When we arrived back home. I found that I could hardly open the door because the vine had grown across it and over the roof. I have brought some of it here to show you.

This passage of scripture describes God as a gardener who tends his vines. It tells us that he chops off the branches that are not bearing any fruit and then prunes back the branches that bear fruit so that the vine will bear even better fruit. Our own vine has used up all its energy growing leaves and you can see that the fruit is very feeble. To have better fruit we must prune back the leaves so that the sun can reach the fruit to ripen it.

But what does all this have to do with us. Well Jesus says that he is like the vine and we are like the branches. This means that all the strength, all the hope and faith, all the love we need to be able to live our lives well and fruitfully comes through him and flows into us. Our job as branches is simply to stay attached to him so that his life can come flowing in and through us. Jesus talks about remaining in him or abiding in him. I know that many of you have been with Jesus a very long time, some of you for the whole of your lives. You have remained faithful to the Lord and persevered in your faith through all the ups and downs of life and you have experienced the faithfulness of the Lord to you too. As I have got to know you and heard something of the story of your lives, I have seen how fruitful you have been. Many of you have been very fruitful in your family lives, in your working lives and in your lives as part of church communities and neighbourhoods.

But what about our lives here? Well we remain in Jesus when we gather with others as we are now to worship and pray together. But also, we stay close to Jesus in our quiet times of prayer in our own rooms. We receive Jesus' life when we make choices to reach out to others in love, to forgive, to be generous. But also, when we just relax and know in the quietness of our own hearts that God loves us and that we belong to him. Our lives here can be meaningful and fruitful as we live together here and as together, we build a community of love and faith.
Our next hymn; In heavenly love abiding is about the peace that comes to us when we stay close to Jesus and put our hope and trust in him.

Prayers

So, as we come now to our time of prayer, let us pray that we will remain close to Jesus and through him live fruitful lives. Let us pray.

Lord Jesus you are the vine and we are the branches, please help us to abide in you for the rest of our lives. May we know how close you are to us. Lord in your mercy....

We ask that all the hope, faith and love we need to live our lives fruitfully and meaningfully would come flowing from you to us each day. Lord in your mercy.....

We pray for all those who care for us here that you would bless them and their families and that you would fill them with all the love, gentleness and compassion they need for this work. Lord in your mercy....

We pray for all those known to us who are suffering in any way in body, mind or spirit. Please bring them your comfort, peace and healing. Lord in your mercy....

We pray for all the troubled places of our world, where there is war, famine or natural disaster please bring your justice and peace and be close to those who suffer. Lord in your mercy.....

Let us draw all these prayers together in the words of the **Lord's Prayer.**

The Workers in the Vineyard

Picture: The workers in the vineyard by The Benedictine
                                        Nuns of Turvey Abbey

Welcome and Introduction

Opening Response:

Leader: Coming and going
All: **God watches over us**

Leader: Resting and waiting
All: **God watches over us**

Leader: In good times and bad times
All: **God watches over us**

Leader: All the days of our lives
All: **God watches over us**

Hymn: Praise my soul

Let us confess our sin:

Leader: Lord forgive us
All: **Lord forgive us and help us.**

For the times we have forgotten to love you and give you
thanks for all your goodness. Lord forgive us….

For the times we have been unkind or forgotten to love those
around us. Lord forgive us…..

Lord forgive us and help us to love you and our neighbours
that we might grow together as a community of love and faith.
Amen

Reading: Matthew 20: 1-16

Talk

Hymn: Great is thy faithfulness

Prayers
Leader: Lord in your mercy
All: **Hear our prayer**

Let us draw all these prayers together in the words of
The Lord's Prayer

All: **Our Father who art in Heaven......**

Hymn: Be thou my vision

Closing Responses:

Leader: We are God's people
                Loved and cherished
All: **We go out in joy**

Leader: We are God's people
                Called and challenged
All: **We go out in joy**

Leader: We are God's people
                Refreshed and forgiven
                We go out in joy

All: **The Grace**

Talk

This is a story that Jesus told, about some men who were hired to work in a vineyard. I know just a little bit about vines because I have one in my garden at home. I have brought a little bit of my vineyard to show you.

One of the things I know is that the way we are growing our vine is not at all the correct way! In about June it goes absolutely mad and grows so fast all over the back of our house that if we go on holiday at that time when we arrive home, we have to cut our way out of the back door!

If any of you have ever been to the wine producing regions of France, you will have seen how it really should be done. Vines are grown on sunny hillsides where there is no shade. Vines are grown up little posts which are only so high, and they are planted in rows which run on for miles and miles. When my husband was a student, he spent some summers, grape picking and he said to me that it is back breaking work and very hot out in the full sun. He spent long days walking along the rows of vines and stooping to pick the grapes.

Well this is what our workers were doing. It was the custom in those days for labourers to hire themselves out for a day at a time and they would go early in the morning to the market place and hope to get some work. So, the vineyard owner goes along to the market place to hire some men for grape picking and he agrees to pay them the going rate for a day's work. However, as the day goes on he realises that he needs more workers, so he ends up going back to the market place several times. This means that some of his workers have done a 12-hour shift in the hot sun, some 9 hours, some 6 hours, some 3 hours and some only 1 hour. The time comes for the workers to be paid and they all line up and the vineyard owner makes his way up the line paying the workers. And he does an extraordinary thing. He pays those who have only worked for an hour a full day's pay. Everyone in the line is looking and wondering what they will be paid. They are astonished when they realise, they are all being paid the same. We can imagine the reaction. Its not fair! We've been walking stooping, picking, slaving in the hot sun for 12 hours, they have only worked 1 hour and in the cool of the day. We want justice! We want more money!

We have to remember the reason why Jesus told these parables. It was to give us some understanding of what God is like. So, what does it tell us about God? Does this story tell us that God is not fair?

The vineyard owner knew that all those workers had their wives, children and parents at home and that they were waiting for the days wages to be able to put food on the table. He had agreed a full day's wage with the workers that worked all day, but then he chose to be generous and compassionate with all the rest, giving them what they needed for their families even though they had only worked a short while for him.

But what does this story say to us here. Well many of us here are like the workers who have been working all day. We have been serving God for the whole of our lives. We have served him in our families, in our churches, in our places of work and in our service of humanity. Others of us have started serving God much later in life and others only right at the end of our lives. But the focus here is not on the length of service but on God's compassion and generosity and that at the end of our lives all of us will be welcome to receive the same reward to spend eternity with the one we have loved and served.

The next hymn; Great is thy faithfulness is about God's faithfulness, his mercy and love towards us throughout our lives. It is never too late to open our hearts to him to receive his generous gift.

Prayers

As we come now to our time of prayer let us give thanks for the time that we have known and loved the Lord however long or short a time it is. Lord in your mercy…..

Heavenly Father, we thank you for your great generosity and love and for the privilege it is to give our lives in service of you. Please give us your strength to keep serving you in one another here. Lord in your mercy…

We thank you for the loving service of all those who care for us here, for the staff and volunteers and for our families and friends. May they be generous in giving themselves to this work and may they be filled with your love and compassion. Lord in your mercy….

We also thank you for the generosity of all those from the local churches who come to serve here, may they be blessed in their work among us. Lord in your mercy….

We pray for all those who are suffering in any way in body, mind or spirit and for all those in hospital at this time. May they know your comfort, healing and peace. Lord in your mercy…..

Let us draw all these prayers together in the words of the **Lord's Prayer.**

REMEMBRANCE

Marking the Season of Remembrance

Introduction

The month of November is traditionally a time to remember. We remember those who lost their lives in the World Wars and our loved ones who have gone before us. We may also want to remember beloved residents who have passed away during the past year. The mood is sombre, reflective and respectful.

Most of our residents were children during World War II, some of the very oldest ones were in active service. Their parents may have been in the armed services or engaged in war work. They can remember the air raid shelters, the gas masks, rationing. Those who lived in London or Coventry can remember the Blitz. Many left school at age 14 and went into some sort of war work. Some of them have parents or grandparents who fought and were lost in World War I. These people are the last generation who can remember the war and they connect us with an important period in the history of our nation. This season of remembrance gives those of us who are younger the opportunity to listen to and learn from the memories, stories and wisdom of this amazingly resilient generation.

Our services during this season allow us to share some of these stories and memories, to honour the lives of this generation of people for their sacrifice which has brought us so many years of peace in the UK and Europe and which helped to rebuild our nation after the war.

This season also gives us the opportunity to think about and remember all those who have loved and nurtured us in life and all those who have helped us to grow in faith and to give thanks for all they have meant to us. It is a time to draw strength from the hope our faith gives us, that death is not the end, but that Jesus has gone before us to prepare a place for us and for our loved ones with whom we will one day be reunited.

Most residents, even those with dementia seem to understand the solemnity of the occasion, but we have found it useful to have the two minutes silence from the BBC on a screen so that they have something to look at which helps those who are easily distracted. We use broadcasts on You Tube if we are doing the service on another day. We also often find that staff want to attend the Remembrance Service and can sometimes be very moved by it - so it is good to be prepared for some emotion in the room. Some residents may want to wear items of uniform or medals to mark the occasion and this adds to its meaning.

We like to do Remembrance Services on or close to 11th November but then continue with a theme of remembering throughout the month of November.

Paris Prayer

Help us tread gently in our night of sorrow
Seeing the kindness in the eyes of strangers
And the sadness in the eyes of friends
May we fight division with unity
Falsehood with truth
And hatred with love.
Guide those who lead us and seek to protect us,
That together we might more faithfully reflect the compassionate
Courage of the One who loved us and gave himself for us.
'Til morning comes and shadows fly away.
Amen

191

Planning Remembrance Services

Mood and atmosphere: Sombre, reverent, respectful, prayerful

Colours: Red

Visual display: Poppy Wreath

Candle

War time photos, medals, memorabilia

Theme, Story, Message: We will remember them - memories of those lost in the war

We will remember them - all our departed loved ones

God will never forget us

Bible Readings: Rom 8:35,37-39,   Heb 12:1-2, Rev 21: 1-5, Is 49: 14-16

Hymns: I vow to thee my country

Jerusalem

O God our help in ages past

Make me a channel of your peace

The day thou gavest

Taize- Jesus remember them

For all the saints

Fight the good fight

Be thou my vision

The Act of Remembrance: They shall not grow old ......

.......we will remember them

Prayers: Prayer of St. Francis - Make me a channel

Paris Prayer

We will remember them -

Mike Stanley (You Tube video)

Visual aids and 3D Activities: Residents wearing items of uniform and medals

Write down or record residents memories

Displays of war time photos

War time memorabilia

193

Remembrance Day Service

Visual display: Poppy wreath, cross, candle

Two minutes silence from the BBC 11/11/15
(live or on You Tube)

Welcome and Introduction

Opening Responses

Leader: Let us remember before God and commend to His
sure and safe keeping all those who have died for
their country in war and all who have lived and died
in the service of mankind.

They shall not grow old
As we who are left grow old
Age will not weary them
Nor the years condemn
At the going down of the sun
And in the morning

All: **We will remember them**

Hymn: I vow to thee my country

Let us remember that peace in our world begins with you and
me. Let us pray that we might be peacemakers

Prayer of St. Francis
Lord, make me an instrument of your peace
Where there is hatred, let me sow love;
Where there is injury pardon;
Where there is doubt, faith;
Where there is darkness, light
And where there is sadness, joy.

Talk

Reading: Romans 8:35, 37-39

Hymn: Be thou my vision

Prayers:

  YouTube: Video clip to lead into the prayers: Mike Stanley - We will remember.

Leader: Lord we pray to you
All: **Taize Chant:**

              Jesus remember them
              When you come into your kingdom
              Jesus remember them
              When they come into your kingdom

Let us draw all these prayers together in the words of
The Lord's Prayer

All: **Our Father who art in Heaven……**

Hymn: Jerusalem

Blessing: May the Lord bless us and keep us
                  May the Lord make his face to shine upon us
                  And be gracious to us
                  May the Lord lift up the light of his countenance
                  on us and give us his peace. **Amen**

All: **The Grace**

Talk

Some of you will remember that over the last couple of weeks ago we have been coming around with a notebook and asking you to tell us about your memories of the war. Most of you were children or teenagers during World War II and so you are the last generation of people to have lived through it and can remember it. That makes you very special! In this room we have a kind of living history. It is so important that those of us who are younger and haven't lived through the war listen to you and learn something from what you share with us. We have tried to capture your memories in a display of memories and poems which you might like to have a look at and find out about different people's experiences of the war years.

So, what have I learned through listening to you? I was struck by the fact that most of you left school at 14 and went straight into some form of war work which seems young to us today. I have a 14-year-old son of my own and it is hard to imagine him working long days in a factory as many of you did. Some of you who were a little older were called up and served in the forces. Some of you got married during the war and told me how you managed to put on a wedding when there was rationing. Some of you who were younger were evacuated from the cities or if you lived in the countryside you can remember having evacuees from the cities come to your schools. You have told me about coupons and rationing and the scarcity of food and basic items. You have told me about the air raids and having to sleep at night in air raid shelters or in the London Underground on the platforms.

But as I have listened to you I have found myself really admiring a certain sort of resilience that I see in you. One of you said to me that you believed that living through the difficulties of the war years has given you the strength to go through other difficult times in your life. Several others have talked to me about your resilience as children just being able to get on with it and somehow to bounce back and still enjoy life despite the nights spent in air raid shelters. I have heard about the camaraderie between neighbours during those years, the sharing of the little you had with one another and helping one another when in danger. I am impressed at the tremendous war effort in this country and the way that everyone pulled together.

And so, the reading I have chosen today which I think best expresses what you have shared with me is from Romans 8: 35-37

Hymn: Be thou my vision

Prayers:

Leader: Lord we pray to you

All: **Jesus remember them......**

As we come to this time of prayer, we especially remember all those who contributed in anyway to the war effort and who secured for us freedom and peace.

Heavenly Father on this Remembrance Day, we remember all those who died in the two world wars, not just our own British people but all those the world over who lost their lives.
Lord we pray to you......

We pray for all those currently serving in the armed forces and involved in conflicts in Syria, Afghanistan and in the Middle East. Please protect them and keep them and all innocent people safe and may there be a speedy end to these conflicts. Lord we pray to you....

We pray for all those working for peace in our world. Please help them through dialogue and understanding, through forgiveness and reconciliation to come to peaceful solutions.
Lord we pray to you....

We draw all these prayers together in the words of **The Lord's Prayer**

Service of Remembering I

Welcome and Introduction

Opening Responses:

Leader: For all our loved ones gone before us we give thanks and

All: **We will remember them**

Leader: For all those who have nurtured us and helped us to grow in faith, we give thanks and

All: **We will remember them**

Leader: For all those who have shared our life here we give thanks, and

All: **We will remember them**

Hymn: Fight the good fight

Let us confess our sin:

Leader: Lord forgive us
All: **Lord forgive us and help us.**

For the times we have forgotten to love you and give you thanks for all your goodness. Lord forgive us....

For the times we have been unkind or forgotten to love those around us. Lord forgive us.....

Lord forgive us and help us to love you and our neighbours that we might grow together as a community of love and faith.

Reading: Hebrews 12:1-2

Talk

Hymn: For all the saints

Prayers:

Leader: Lord we pray to you
All: **Taize Chant**
                   Jesus remember them when you come into
                   your Kingdom

Let us draw all these prayers together in the words of
The Lord's Prayer

Hymn: Be thou my vision

Blessing:
                   Faint not nor fear, his arm is near
                   He changes not, and you are dear
                   Only believe and you shall see
                   That Christ is all in all to thee.

All: **The Grace**

Talk

This Bible passage from the book of Hebrews is asking us to imagine our Christian life as a race. It describes a race track with a finishing line somewhere ahead. It describes a great crowd of people either side of the track who are cheering and shouting and waving banners for those who are running. But who are they? What is this great cloud of witnesses? We can only answer this question by going back to the previous chapter. Chapter 11 is a great long list of many of the people of faith who appear in the Old Testament part of the Bible. There are people such as Noah and Abraham, Joseph and Moses, Gideon, Samuel and David.

So, we know that as we run our own particular race through this life we have those people of faith to inspire and encourage us. But the list of people of faith does not stop there. We have all the people of the New Testament as well, people like Mary and Elisabeth, Peter and Paul and the other apostles and many more.

But the list does not stop there either. Because after them we have had 2000 years of the church with many other notable people who are remembered by the church and that list goes on and on to the present day.

Today I would like us to think about all the special people in our own lives who have died and gone before us. We are going to have a moment's quiet and I would like you to think back over your life and to remember any special people who have really helped you to grow in faith or to keep going when things were tough. They could be parents, spouses, members of your family. They could be Sunday School teachers, ministers, other people at church, god parents, friends, strangers, any one who has kept you going in your own faith journey.
Let's just think for a moment.

Have you all thought of someone?

Now I am going to read the passage again. As I read it I want you to imagine yourself running the race. Imagine the great crowd who are cheering for you to keep going. In the crowd imagine the faces of your own special people encouraging you to keep going, keep fixing your eyes on Jesus.

Read the passage – Hebrews 12:1-2

Life can sometimes be very hard, and I don't know about you, but I find this passage very comforting because it tells us that our loved ones who have gone before us, are not far away. They are in fact very close, praying for us, encouraging us to keep going and to keep looking at Jesus.

Prayers

Leader: Lord we pray to you
All: **Jesus remember them when you come into your kingdom**

As we come to our time of prayer let us remember that we are joining our prayers with the continuous prayer of all those people of faith who have gone before us.

Heavenly Father, today we give thanks for all our loved ones who have gone before us. We thank you for the lives we lived together, the love and friendship we shared and all that we gave and received from one another. We pray that you will keep them safe in your love until we meet again. Lord we pray to you……

Today we particularly remember all those who have given us the gift of faith, those who have helped to nurture and grow our faith and those who have helped us to persevere in faith through the ups and downs of life. We thank you for their faithfulness and encouragement. Lord we pray to you….

We thank you for our family here and pray that we may continually be built into a community of love and faith, a place where we can help and encourage one another to grow and keep running the race. Lord we pray to you…..

Let us draw all these prayers together in the words of the **Lord's Prayer.**

Service of Remembering II

Welcome and Introduction

Opening Responses

Leader: For all our loved ones gone before us we give
            thanks and
All: **We will remember them**

Leader: For all those who have nurtured us and helped us
            to grow in faith, we give thanks and
All: **We will remember them**

Leader: For all those who have shared our life here we give
            thanks, and
All: **We will remember them**

Hymn: O God our help in ages past

Let us confess our sin:

Leader: Lord forgive us
 All: **Lord forgive us and help us.**

For the times we have forgotten to love you and give you
thanks for all your goodness. Lord forgive us….

For the times we have been unkind or forgotten to love those
around us. Lord forgive us…..

Lord forgive us and help us to love you and our neighbours
that we might grow together as a community of love and faith.

Reading: Rev. 7: 9,13-17

Talk

Hymn: For all the saints

Prayers
Leader: Lord we pray to you
All: **Jesus remember them when you come into your kingdom.**

Let us draw all these prayers together in the words of
The Lord's Prayer

All: **Our Father who art in Heaven……**

Hymn: The day thou gavest

Blessing: May the Lord bless us and keep us
May the Lord make his face to shine upon us
And be gracious to us
May the Lord lift up the light of his countenance
on us and give us his peace
Amen

All: **The Grace**

Introduction to the service

Well here we are in November already. I don't know about you, but I keep asking myself where this year has gone. November is traditionally a time for remembering, it is a more reflective season which is sandwiched between the joyful seasons of Harvest and Christmas. It is a time to remember in a special way our loved ones who have gone before us and to remember those who lost their lives because of war. Before the service today I came around to see most of you and put the names of the people you would like to remember today on these poppies. So, this is our Remembrance tree which contains the names of the people we want to remember throughout the month of November. Also, today we will be remembering our friends at this care home who have passed away this last year and giving thanks for them.

Reading: Rev. 7: 9,13-17

Talk

This is a wonderful reading that many of our churches would have had for All Saints last Sunday. It describes the vision of John in Revelation of a great crowd of people all dressed in white. These are all the people who have gone before us including our own loved ones. There they are perfectly happy at the throne of God serving him and praying for us. All their suffering has come to an end they are at peace. One day at the right time all of us will join them there with Jesus and be reunited with our loved ones never to be parted again. This is the hope our faith gives us.

Prayers

Leader: We will remember them
All: Jesus remember them

As we come to our time of prayer let us remember that we are joining our prayers with the continuous prayer of all those people of faith who have gone before us.

Heavenly Father, today we give thanks for all our loved ones who have gone before us, husbands, wives, children, parents, grandparents, sisters, brothers and other family members, friends and neighbours. We thank you for the lives we lived together, the love and friendship we shared and all that we gave and received from one another. We pray that you will keep them safe in your love until we meet again.
We will remember them, **Jesus remember them**.....

Today we particularly remember all those who have given us the gift of faith, those who have helped to nurture and grow our faith and those who have helped us to persevere in faith through the ups and downs of life. Parents and godparents, school and Sunday School teachers, youth workers, house group leaders and ministers. We thank you for their faithfulness and encouragement.
We will remember them, **Jesus remember them**....

We thank you for our community here and pray that we may continually encourage one another to keep growing in love and faith. Especially today we remember our friends who have passed away in this past year.
We will remember them, **Jesus remember them**.....

Let us include ourselves in this prayer as we sing another couple of times, **Jesus remember me**.....

The Lord's Prayer

Engraved on the palm of God's hand

Welcome and Introduction

Can a mother forget the baby at her breast and have no compassion on the child she has borne? Though she may forget, I will not forget you! See, I have engraved you on the palms of my hands.(Is:49)

Opening response:

Leader:	Shine in our lives
	Warm us with courage
All:	**Keep us close to you**
Leader:	Shine in our lives
	Light up our darkness
All:	**Keep us close to you**
Leader:	Shine in our lives
	Raise us to glory
All:	**Keep us close to you**
Hymn:	Blessed assurance

Confession
Leader:	Lord forgive us
All:	**Lord forgive us and help us.**

Lord Jesus we come before you today just as we are with our strengths and weaknesses, our doubts and fears, our joys and sorrows.

For the times when we have closed ourselves to God and not loved him with all our heart. Lord forgive us….

For the times when we have closed ourselves to one another and not loved one another fully. Lord forgive us…

May God our Father forgive us and help us to love him and our neighbours here, that we might continue to grow together as a community of love and faith. **Amen**

Reading: Isaiah 49: 14 - 16

Talk

Hymn: Kum ba yah

Prayers:
Leader: Lord in your mercy
All: **Hear our prayer**

Let us draw all these prayers together in the words of
The Lord's Prayer

All: **Our Father who art in Heaven……**

Hymn: He's got the whole world

Blessing:

                  God says to us…..
                  I have loved you with an everlasting love
                  I will never leave you nor forsake you
                  I will never forget you
                  So, may God bless us and keep us safe in the
                  palm of his hand. Amen

All: **The Grace**

Talk

First of all, it might seem a bit of a personal question, but does anyone here have a tattoo? Tattoos are words or pictures which are inked onto the skin and can't be removed. Once a tattoo is there it will be there for the whole of your life. You might have seen people who have the name of someone who is very special and important to them. Even you see quite tough looking men with the word MUM on their arm or it might be their wife or girlfriend or their child. But whoever it is that name will be on their body forever, that person is so special and important to them that they never want to forget them, they want to be constantly reminded of them.

Our Bible reading today is only very short, but it is a wonderful message from God. He is telling us that he has a tattoo. It's surprising isn't it? We perhaps wouldn't expect God to have a tattoo. And what is even more surprising is that his tattoo is your name. Did you know that God has your name engraved on the palm of his hand? This means that God is constantly reminded of you. He can never forget you. Also, it means that your name is there on his hand forever, it can never be removed. He has been with you all through your life, he has not forgotten you and even now that you are here in this care home, you are still on his mind, he knows you are here. He is thinking about you. You are special and important to him.

Listen again to the Bible verse which is the words of God spoken to us.....

Prayers

As we come to our time of prayer, we thank God that he has not forgotten us, but he knows we are here and he is here with us.

Heavenly Father, we thank you that you have an amazing memory, that you know us by name and that you have our names engraved on the palm of your hand. Thank you that we are special and important to you and that you love us so much. Lord in your mercy....

We pray for all those who care for us here, for staff and managers and volunteers. We thank you for their tender care of us and we pray that they too would know how much you love them and how precious they are to you. Lord in your mercy.....

We pray for all those known to us and those we don't know, who feel lost or afraid, lonely or unwell. Please be close to them, let them know that you haven't forgotten them, but that you love them. May they feel your tender love surround them at this time. Lord in your mercy....

Let us draw all these prayers together in the words of the **Lord's Prayer.**

ORDINARY TIME

Introduction to 'Ordinary time'

Ordinary Time makes up the parts of the year that are in between the special times of celebration. The colour green is often used during these times of the year to represent a time of growth in the life of a Christian.

The services offered in this part of the book are to help residents to grow in faith to grow in their understanding of the Christian life and be challenged to live it out in their present stage of life and circumstances, to encounter Jesus in the Biblical stories and to respond to his call. They include themes of; responding to the call to follow Jesus; being part of God's family; a series of three services on prayer some of Jesus' parables about the Kingdom of God, some encounters of people with Jesus.

These services are presented roughly in the order that their themes appear in the gospels, but they can be used in any order and at any time in the year although certain themes such as the feeding of the five thousand and the wedding at Cana lend themselves to services during the summer.

On the next page is a blank template to help you plan your services. Hymns and songs are suggested which help to reinforce the message you want to communicate.

Planning services during 'Ordinary Time'

Mood and atmosphere:

Colours: Green

Visual display: Green table cloth, cross, Bible, candle, flowers,

Theme, Story, Message:

Bible Readings:

Hymns:

Prayers:

Visual aids and 3D Activities:

The calling of the first disciples

Picture: The calling of the first disciples by The Benedictine
Nuns of Turvey Abbey

Welcome and Introduction

Jesus said "Come follow me and I will make you fishers of men."   *(Matt 4:19)*

Opening Responses:

Leader: The Lord is here among us
All: **He calls us by name**

Leader: The Lord loves us
All: **He calls us by name**

Leader: The Lord is always with us
All: **He calls us by name**

Hymn: Dear Lord and Father

Confession:
Leader: Lord forgive us
All: **Lord forgive us and help us.**

Lord Jesus we come before you today just as we are with our
strengths and weaknesses, our doubts and fears, our joys and
sorrows.

For the times when we have closed ourselves to God and not
loved him with all of our heart. Lord forgive us….

For the times when we have closed ourselves to one another and not loved one another fully. Lord forgive us…

May God our Father forgive us and help us to love him and our neighbours that we might grow together as a community of love and faith. **Amen**

Reading: Matthew 4: 18-22

Talk:

Hymn: I want to walk with Jesus Christ

Prayers:
Leader: Lord in your mercy
All: **Hear our prayer**

Let us draw all these prayers together in the words of
The Lord's Prayer

All: **Our Father who art in Heaven…**

Hymn: Blessed assurance

Blessing**:**

                    May the Lord bless us and keep us

                    May the Lord make his face to shine upon us
                    and be gracious to us

                    May the Lord lift up the light of his countenance
                    on us and give us his peace. Amen

All: **The Grace**

Talk

Matt: 4: 18-22

In this story, Jesus is right at the beginning of his public ministry. He has begun to preach and to heal people and one day he is walking along beside the Sea of Galilee and he sees two brothers – Simon and Andrew.
Here they are in the picture with their nets ready to go out fishing.

Then an extraordinary thing happens – Jesus speaks to them and says
"Come follow me and I will make you fishers of men."

Does anyone know what happened next?

They left everything - their nets, their fishing boats, their jobs as fishermen, their families, their homes and they followed Jesus.
Jesus had not told them what would happen – where they would sleep, how they would live, what they would do, if they would get paid. All he said was,
"Come and follow me and I will make you fishers of men."

I wonder why these brothers just left everything and followed Jesus?

I think that they had been listening to him and they realised that he was completely different from their religious leaders. He told them that God was their Father and that they were his children. He spoke of a new way of living that involves trusting God to provide and that they could simply talk to God and ask him for what they needed. He told them of a special way of love that involved loving God and loving their neighbours.

I think that when Simon and Andrew heard Jesus speak they were somehow attracted by this new way of life and so when Jesus invites then to follow him they were ready to leave everything behind and set out on a kind of adventure. And the three years that followed certainly were an adventure.

I wonder if any of you have heard Jesus call to you in your life – "Come follow me." I'm going to tell you about when Jesus first called me to come follow him………

(Speaker or member of the team tells their own story)

We are never too young or never too old to follow Jesus and all it needs is a very simple prayer – Lord Jesus please come into my heart and help me to follow you all my life.

Hymn: I want to walk with Jesus Christ.

Prayers

As we come to our time of prayer we remember that Jesus is with us now and he is saying to us, "Come follow me."
If you have never heard Jesus' call to you before and you would like to respond then please pray this prayer in your heart as I say the words…..

Lord Jesus thank you for calling me to follow you. Please Lord Jesus would you come into my heart and help me to follow you. Amen.

Lord Jesus thank you that you are with us here every moment and we pray that you will help us to live for you and to share your love with one another here in this place. Amen.

The Lord's Prayer

What do you want me to do for you?
Jesus' teaching on prayer

Visual display: Begging bowl with a few coins.

Welcome and Introduction

Jesus asked the blind beggar, "What do you want me to do for you?"
(Luke 18:41)

Opening Responses:

Leader:	Round about us
	Here among us
All:	**God of promise and love**

Leader:	Good and faithful
	Strong in mercy
All:	**God of promise and love**

Leader:	Calling our names
	Bidding us welcome
All:	**God of promise and love**

Hymn: Amazing grace

Confession:

Leader:	Lord forgive us
All:	**Lord forgive us and help us.**

Lord Jesus we come before you today just as we are with our strengths and weaknesses, our doubts and fears, our joys and sorrows.

For the times when we have closed ourselves to God and not loved him with all our heart. Lord forgive us….

For the times when we have closed ourselves to one another and not loved one another fully. Lord forgive us…

May God our Father forgive us and help us to love him and our neighbours that we might grow together as a community of love and faith. **Amen**

Reading: Luke 18:35 - 43

Talk:

Hymn: Be still for the presence

Prayers:

Leader: Lord in your mercy
All: **Hear our prayer**

Let us draw all these prayers together in the words of
The Lord's Prayer

All: **Our Father who art in Heaven…**

Hymn: Great is thy faithfulness

Blessing:

                     Lay your hands gently upon us
                     Let your touch render your peace
                     Let them bring your forgiveness and healing
                     Lay your hands gently lay your hands.

                     May God bless us and keep us and hold us
                     in the palm of his hands. **Amen.**

All: **The Grace**

Talk

Luke 18: 35-43

This is the story of a blind beggar who spent his days sitting by the roadside with a begging bowl in his hand. In those days there were no services for the blind, no social services, no welfare payments. This man was not able to work so the only way for him to live was to beg and to rely on the sympathy and compassion of those who passed by him.

But one day something very different happens. Jesus is coming along the road surrounded by a big crowd of people. The beggar must have heard stories about Jesus and the things he was doing. I think he must have felt some hope rising within him. Perhaps he thought to himself this is my only chance I must take it. So he starts to cry out at the top of his voice, "Jesus son of David have mercy on me!" The crowd try to shut him up but he becomes even more persistent "Jesus son of David have mercy on me!" Jesus stops and calls the man over and asks him a very important question. Can anyone remember what the question was that Jesus asks the man?

"What is it you want me to do for you?"
Can anyone remember the man's reply?

The man replies very simply, "I want to see."
Jesus puts his hands on the man's eyes and he is able to see.

It is a lovely story, but what does it say to us here?
In this story Jesus is teaching us very simply how to pray. He asks us that same question, "What is it you would like me to do for you?" I wonder if you have ever thought how you would reply if Jesus stood before you now and asked you that question.

He is asking you to think now what do I really need Jesus to do for me. Is there something on my mind, in my heart, something happening to me at the moment that I really want to ask Jesus to help me with.

I would like you to think about that question as we sing our next hymn:
Be still for the presence of the Lord.

Prayers

In a few quiet moments let us listen to Jesus' question to us, "What do you want me to do for you?" In the quietness of your own heart simply tell Jesus what you need.....

Lord Jesus we thank you that you are here with us now, and that you know each one of us and care for us. We bring before you all these prayers spoken in the quietness of our hearts but heard by you. Lord in your mercy.....

We pray for all our loved ones, our families and friends and all those who care for us and support us. Please be close to them and give me your strength and peace. Lord in your mercy

We pray for all those who care for us here, for the staff and volunteers and for the managers. Please fill them with gentleness and kindness and joy in their work. Lord in your mercy...

We pray for all those known to us who are suffering in anyway in body, mind and spirit. Especially we pray for the refugees. We pray for peace and healing in all the troubled places of our world. Lord in your mercy......

The Lord's Prayer

Our Father
Lord teach us to pray

Welcome and Introduction

One day Jesus was praying in a certain place. When he had finished his disciples said to him, "Lord teach us to pray." (Luke 11:1)

Opening Responses:

Leader:	Round about us
	Here among us
All:	**God of promise and love**
Leader:	Good and faithful
	Strong in mercy
All:	**God of promise and love**
Leader:	Calling our names
	Bidding us welcome
All:	**God of promise and love**

Hymn: 333   'All my Hope on God is founded

Confession:

Leader:	Lord forgive us
All:	**Lord forgive us and help us.**

Lord Jesus we come before you today just as we are with our strengths and weaknesses, our doubts and fears, our joys and sorrows.

For the times when we have closed ourselves to God and not loved him with all of our heart. Lord forgive us....

For the times when we have closed ourselves to one another and not loved one another fully. Lord forgive us…

May God our Father forgive us and help us to love him and our neighbours that we might grow together as a community of love and faith. **Amen**

Reading: Luke 11:1,2 Matt 6: 5-13

Talk:

Hymn: 440 *Praise to the Lord, the Almighty, the King of Creation*

Prayers:
Leader: Lord in your mercy
All: **Hear our prayer**

Let us draw all these prayers together in the words of
The Lord's Prayer

All: **Our Father who art in Heaven…**

Hymn: 285 *For the Beauty of the Earth*

Blessing:

Jesus said, "Ask and it will be given to you; seek and you will find; knock and the door will be opened to you. For everyone who asks receives, he who seeks finds and to him who knocks, the door will be opened. May God bless us and keep us and hold us in the palm of his hands.

All: **The Grace**

Introduction to the service

In our service last week we were telling the story of the blind beggar calling out to Jesus, "Lord Jesus, Son of David, have mercy on me."
Jesus stops to talk to him and asks him a very important question.
"What do you want me to do for you?"
The blind man knew exactly what he wanted and said "I want to see."

I was saying last week that in fact Jesus is teaching us how to pray. That when we pray we can imagine that Jesus is standing right here in front of us asking that question, "What do you want me to do for you?" And then we ask ourselves what I really need from God today and then simply tell him what we need.
In our service today we are going to learn a little bit more about prayer.

Talk

Today our reading begins with Jesus praying. Clearly the way he was praying was something different from the way the religious leaders prayed and perhaps different from the way that the disciples had been taught to pray when they were children because the disciples say to Jesus "Lord teach us to pray....."

Jesus then teaches them a very simple way of praying which we now know as The Lord's Prayer. Probably all of you were taught this prayer when you were young perhaps at home – you may have knelt by the bed at night and prayed it, perhaps you said it at school or at Sunday School, perhaps you taught it to your own children. Do you know that Jesus taught his disciples this prayer more than 2000 years ago and here we are still praying it today!
(Speaker can ask residents and team members where and when they learned the Lord's Prayer, listen to the stories)

Song

Let's sing it together, Our Father who art in heaven.....

We know it so well, but what does it mean?

Jesus taught us to call God Father. He wants us to know that we have a loving Father who listens to us and who cares for us. God is our Father and we are his children. Have you ever thought to yourself, God is my Father and I am a son, a daughter of God that sounds special doesn't it?

Hallowed be thy name – your name is holy. It is a precious, special name.

Your kingdom come, your will be done on earth as it is in Heaven.
We are praying that the earth where we live would become like Heaven where God lives. The earth would become a place where there is goodness and love and great happiness and where we can live together in peace.

Give us today our daily bread – Father please give us everything we need.

Forgive us for the things we have done wrong and we will forgive others who have wronged us in some way. This is part of Jesus' prayer because it can harm us and make us unhappy to hold bitterness in our hearts towards others. Forgiveness helps us to live in peace with one another.

Keep us safe from the evil one and protect us from all harm.

Song

Let us sing the song again..... Our Father...
And as we do think about the words and what they mean.

Prayers

As we come to our time of prayer, let us remember that God is our loving Father and that we are his precious children. God loves us to come and talk to him in prayer.

We pray for our world which is full of trouble. People suffer because of war, lack of food and water and poverty. We pray that our world would become a place of goodness and love, happiness and peace. Lord in your mercy.....

We pray that you would provide everything we need in our daily lives and particularly we pray for those who are poor, homeless, unemployed and who struggle to make ends meet. Lord in your mercy.....

We pray for all those who have wronged us in whatever way. Please help us to forgive them. Please forgive us too for any harm we may have done to others. Lord in your mercy....

We pray that you would keep us all safe and protect us and all those we love from all harm. Lord in your mercy......

Let us draw these prayer together as we pray **The Lord's Prayer.....**

Song

Kum ba Yah - A prayer that God would come close to us here

Keep praying, don't give up
Jesus' teaching on prayer

Welcome and Introduction

Jesus told his disciples a parable to show them that they should always pray and not give up. (Luke 18:1)

Opening Responses:

Leader:	Round about us
	Here among us
All:	**God of promise and love**

Leader:	Good and faithful
	Strong in mercy
All:	**God of promise and love**

Leader:	Calling our names
	Bidding us welcome
All:	**God of promise and love**

| **Hymn:** | What a friend we have in Jesus |

Confession:

| Leader: | Lord forgive us |
| **All:** | **Lord forgive us and help us.** |

Lord Jesus we come before you today just as we are with our strengths and weaknesses, our doubts and fears, our joys and sorrows.

For the times when we have closed ourselves to God and not loved him with all our heart. Lord forgive us….

For the times when we have closed ourselves to one another and not loved one another fully. Lord forgive us…

May God our Father forgive us and help us to love him and our neighbours that we might grow together as a community of love and faith. **Amen**

Reading: Luke 11: 5-8
                   Luke 18: 2-8
(Read by two voices, read dramatically or acted out)

Talk:

Hymn: Our Father who art in Heaven

Prayers:
Leader: Lord in your mercy
All: **Hear our prayer**

Let us draw all these prayers together in the words of
The Lord's Prayer

All: **Our Father who art in Heaven…**

Hymn: Lord of all hopefulness

Blessing:

          Jesus said, "Ask and it will be given to you; seek and you will find; knock and the door will be opened to you. For everyone who asks receives, he who seeks finds and to him who knocks, the door will be opened

          May God bless us and keep us and hold us in the palm of his hands.

All: **The Grace**

Talk

In the stories we have just heard or seen acted we meet a man who has had unexpected visitors arrive late at night and he has no food in the house to give them and so he knocks on his neighbour's door to see if he will give him some bread. The neighbour is very annoyed at being woken up at this unearthly hour and tells the man to go away. But the man is very persistent and keeps knocking until the neighbour eventually gets up, not because he wants to help but because he wants to get rid of the man and go back to bed.

The second story is similar. This time it is about a woman who goes to see a judge about an injustice that has happened to her. The judge is not a sympathetic or compassionate person and he refuses to help her, but the woman just keeps on demanding justice until the judge gives way and does something for her. Jesus tells these stories to encourage us to pray for what we need, but not just that, to keep praying, to not give up praying.

I wonder if you have every prayed to God for something you need, or someone you care about and your prayer hasn't been answered, there seems to be no change in the situation you are praying for? I know that this has happened to me. It is so easy to lose heart, to give up, to stop praying. Secretly we might think - God has not heard my prayer, God does not want to help me, or even God doesn't care about me. It can be difficult to keep praying when nothing appears to be happening. But often God is at work in ways that we can't see or don't understand. In these Bible passages Jesus reassures us - don't give up praying, God is not like the judge in the story, he <u>does</u> care about you, he <u>is</u> listening to your prayers, he <u>will</u> answer you when you cry out to him.

He goes on to say " Ask and it will be given to you, seek and you will find, knock and the door will be opened to you."

He also says, "If you who are evil know how to give good gifts to your children, how much more will your heavenly Father give the Holy Spirit to those who ask."

There is a beautiful song whose words express that God hears our prayers and is at work in our lives and the lives of those we pray for. It goes like this….

> God will make a way
> where there seems to be no way
> He works in ways we cannot see
> He will make a way for me
> He will be my guide
> hold me closely to his side
> with love and strength for each new day
> He will make a way, He will make a way.(Don Moen)

Prayers

As we come now to our time of prayer, let us remember that God is listening and hears our prayers, he knows what we need and he cares about us and all those we love.

Heavenly Father, we thank you that you hear us when we pray to you, please help us to keep praying and not give up. Please give us the faith to believe that you are at work in our lives even when our prayers appear not to be answered straight away. Lord in your mercy…..

We pray for ourselves and bring all our needs to you. We ask that you would be close to us and help us and provide all that we need. Lord in your mercy….

We pray for all our loved ones that you would be close to them in all that they are going through, may they know that you are with them, give them your strength and protection. Lord in your mercy..

We pray for all those who have no one to pray for them. May they come to know your tender love for them. Lord in your mercy…..

The Lord's Prayer

Jesus calms the storm

Picture: Jesus calms the storm by The Benedictine Nuns
of Turvey Abbey

Welcome and Introduction
Jesus rebuked the wind and said to the waves, "Peace, be still." (Mark 4:39)

Opening Responses:
Leader: God watches over
                     Our waking and sleeping
All: **Our help comes from God**

Leader: God saves our feet
                     From slipping and stumbling
All: **Our help comes from God**

Leader: God keeps guard
                     Over our comings and our goings
All: **Our help comes from God**

Hymn: *353* Dear Lord and Father

Confession:
Leader: Lord forgive us
All: **Lord forgive us and help us.**

Lord Jesus we come before you today just as we are with our strengths and weaknesses, our doubts and fears, our joys and sorrows.

For the times when we have closed ourselves to God and not loved him with all of our heart. Lord forgive us….

For the times when we have closed ourselves to one another and not loved one another fully. Lord forgive us…

231

May God our Father forgive us and help us to love him and our neighbours that we might grow together as a community of love and faith. **Amen**

Reading: Mark 4: 35-41

Talk:

Hymn: 342 *Breathe on me breath of God*

Prayers:
Leader: Lord in your mercy
All: **Hear our prayer**

Let us draw all these prayers together in the words of
The Lord's Prayer

All: 239 **Our Father who art in Heaven…**

Hymn: Lord of all hopefulness

Blessing:

May the peace of Christ that passes all understanding keep our hearts and minds in the knowledge and love of God and of his son Jesus Christ. And may God bless us and keep us safe in the palm of his hand. **Amen**

All: **The Grace**

Talk

In the story we have just heard, Jesus had spent his day outside in the sun, surrounded by a great crowd of people who were listening to his teaching.

It is now evening time and he is tired, so he suggests to the disciples that they leave the crowd behind, get into their boat and sail across Lake Galilee to the other side. Jesus must have been very tired because he settles down in the bottom of the boat for a sleep.

This picture shows us what happens next. The weather suddenly changes, and the disciples find themselves in the middle of a violent storm. I don't know whether that has ever happened to you perhaps on a beautiful summer day you are out for a picnic or an afternoon on the beach and suddenly the sky becomes black and you've had to pack up in a hurry and make a dash for shelter. Such is the British weather!

The picture shows what it is like, can you see the big waves, the wind blowing Jesus' hair and clothes. You can see that the boat is going down and the disciples are paddling furiously. Have a look at the expressions on their faces, how are they feeling – absolutely terrified.

The extraordinary thing is that Jesus is sleeping. Have you ever wondered how Jesus could have slept through the noise of the storm, the wind roaring, the waves crashing into the boat? How did he do that?

I think that the disciples do all they can to control the boat in the storm and to get themselves to safety, but they just can't do it and so they go and wake Jesus up. They ask him this question; "Don't you care if we drown?"
I think that this is a very important question
"Don't you care if we drown?"

There are other questions as well aren't there? Lord why are you sleeping when we are all working so hard to save ourselves from drowning? Lord why are you sleeping when we are so frightened? Lord why aren't you helping us? Don't you care about us?

I think this story is very important because it is about the storms of life that we all go through. None of us will have had a perfectly calm and peaceful life. We have all been through difficult times when we felt very worried or fearful, perhaps when we felt we were going under. Some of us may not have had Jesus in our boat during our lives and felt that we were battling on alone just trying to cope. Others of us may have had Jesus in our boat but felt that he was somehow silent, not really doing anything for us. The disciples went on for long enough before they went to him.

I have asked myself these questions, why did Jesus sleep in the boat while the disciples were struggling? The answer I have come up with, is that I think Jesus was waiting for them to realise that they couldn't do it alone, that on their own they would drown. He was waiting for them to ask for his help.
We see what happens when they did wake him up and ask him to save them.
Here he is standing up in the middle of the storm completely unafraid. He then commands the storm to be quiet – "Peace be still." The storm does as it's told and becomes calm. When Jesus says to the disciples, "Why were you afraid? Do you still have no faith?" I think he means, "Did you really think I would let you drown? Did you really think I didn't care?"

So, what is this story saying to us today?
I think it's saying that if we are living our lives without Jesus in our boat, we can invite him to come on board and to be with us in all we go through in this life. And if we do have Jesus living in our boat with us, he waits for us to invite him to be part of everything we are doing and specially to ask him for his help when we are struggling. Because when we do ask him for help, extraordinary things can happen, but more than anything he says to us, "Peace, be still." Often, he will give us his peace in the midst of the difficult circumstances we go through. I'm sure many of you here have stories of times when you have prayed and God has answered your prayers sometimes in surprising ways.

Hymn: Be still for the presence of the Lord

Prayers

As we come to this time of prayer, may we remember that Jesus is always with us through all we go through in life. We ask him now to help us and all those we love.

If you have been living your life without Jesus in your boat here is a little prayer you may want to pray.....

Lord Jesus I have been living without you in my life. I realise how much I need you to come and be with me and help me. Please would you come into my life and share in every part of it, the good times and the hard times. Please would always be with me and give me your peace. Lord in your mercy....

If you are going through a stormy, difficult time at the moment then this prayer is for you....

Lord Jesus, you are with me and you know what I am going through at the moment, you know my worries and my fears, my problems. Please help me through this time, give me your strength. Fill my heart with peace as I trust in you. Lord in your mercy....

We pray now for all our loved ones who are going through difficult times.
Lord Jesus please be very close to all those we love, please carry them through their troubles and give them your peace. Lord in your mercy....

We pray for all those in our world who are going through the storms of life, may they know your comfort and your help. Lord in your mercy....

The Lord's Prayer

Do not worry

Welcome and Introduction
Seek first the kingdom of God and his righteousness and all these things will be given to you. (Matt 6: 33)

Opening Responses:

Leader: God watches over
                     Our waking and sleeping
All: **Our help comes from God**

Leader: God saves our feet
                     From slipping and stumbling
All: **Our help comes from God**

Leader: God keeps guard
                     Over our comings and our goings
All: **Our help comes from God**

Hymn: When we walk with the Lord

Confession:

Leader: Lord forgive us
All: **Lord forgive us and help us.**

Lord Jesus we come before you today just as we are with our strengths and weaknesses, our doubts and fears, our joys and sorrows.

For the times when we have closed ourselves to God and not loved him with all of our heart. Lord forgive us….

For the times when we have closed ourselves to one another and not loved one another fully. Lord forgive us…

May God our Father forgive us and help us to love him and our neighbours that we might grow together as a community of love and faith. **Amen**

Reading: Matthew 6: 25 - 34

Talk:

Hymn: Seek ye first

Prayers:
Leader: Lord in your mercy
All: **Hear our prayer**

Let us draw all these prayers together in the words of
The Lord's Prayer

All: **Our Father who art in Heaven…**

Hymn: What a friend we have in Jesus

Blessing:

May the peace of Christ that passes all
understanding keep our hearts and minds in
the knowledge and love of God and of his Son
Jesus Christ. And may God bless us and keep
us safe in the palm of his hand. **Amen**

All: **The Grace**

Talk

In the reading today Jesus is teaching us about not worrying. Put your hand up if you are a bit of a worrier. My hand is up because I am a bit of a worrier at times too. Sometimes I wake up in the night with things going around in my mind – perhaps some of you know what that is like. Jesus is speaking to his disciples about not worrying about the ordinary things of life – what they would eat or drink or wear. I think following Jesus must have been a bit unpredictable, probably the disciples didn't know where they would sleep from night to night or where the next meal would come from. What Jesus was saying to them was that he wanted them to put their total trust in God. He wanted them to believe that God really cared about all the little, ordinary but important details of their lives.

Sometimes people have said to me, 'God isn't interested in me! He has far too many other much more important things to think about than me. Look at all the problems in the world – God is far too busy to notice me!

But this isn't true, the Bible says that God notices everything, he even sees the birds and makes sure that they have enough to eat.

The wonderful thing is that God is here with us in this home. There are quite a lot of us living here, but God knows each one of us by name. He knows all about our lives, the things we have been through. He knows what we need.

He says to us, 'There is no need to worry, put your trust in me because I really care about you.' He also says, 'Don't spend your time worrying about your life, but make it a priority to get to know me. More than anything else spend your time seeking after me.

Let's think about that as we sing our next song: Seek ye first

Prayers

As we come to this time of prayer let us remember that God is here and that he really cares about us.

Lord Jesus we bring all our worries to you now. Thank you that you are with us and you know what we need. Help us to put our trust in you.
Lord in your mercy……

We thank you that you have provided everything we need here, we are safe and comfortable and have food to eat, clothes to wear, a bed to sleep in and people around us who care for us.
Lord in your mercy…..

We pray that we would get to know you better and discover how much you love and care for us.
Lord in your mercy…..

We pray for all those in our country and in our world, who do not have enough to eat, those who are homeless, those who are lonely and who have no one to pray for them, please bring them the help they need through the love of your people.
Lord in your mercy….

The Lord's Prayer

Jesus heals the paralysed man

Picture: Jesus heals the paralysed man
                       by The Benedictine Nuns of Turvey Abbey

Welcome and Introduction

Opening Responses:

Leader:	Round about us
	Here among us
All:	**God of promise and love**

Leader:	Good and faithful
	Strong in mercy
All:	**God of promise and love**

Leader:	Calling our names
	Bidding us welcome
All:	**God of promise and love**

| **Hymn:** | Praise my soul |

Confession:
| Leader: | Lord forgive us |
| **All:** | **Lord forgive us and help us.** |

Lord Jesus we come before you today just as we are with our strengths and weaknesses, our doubts and fears, our joys and sorrows.

For the times when we have closed ourselves to God and not loved him with all our heart. Lord forgive us....

For the times when we have closed ourselves to one another and not loved one another fully. Lord forgive us…

May God our Father forgive us and help us to love him and our neighbours that we might grow together as a community of love and faith. **Amen**

Reading: Luke 5: 17-26

Talk:

Hymn: Be still for the presence

Prayers:

Leader: Lord in your mercy
All: **Hear our prayer**

Let us draw all these prayers together in the words of
The Lord's Prayer

All: **Our Father who art in Heaven…**

Hymn: Praise to the Lord the almighty

Blessing:

         Lay your hands gently upon us
         Let your touch render your peace
         Let them bring your forgiveness and healing
         Lay your hands gently lay your hands.

         May God bless us and keep us and hold us in
         the palm of his hands. **Amen**

All: **The Grace**

Talk

Look at the picture.....

This story is about a wonderful healing miracle that comes early on in Jesus' ministry. However, looking at the picture you can see that Jesus isn't actually in it. In fact the focus of the picture is on the paralysed man and his friends.

And what friends they were!

These friends had brought the man to Jesus for healing. I imagine that it must have been quite an effort to get him there in the first place. There were no wheelchairs or beds on wheels in those days. Somehow they have managed to carry him on his mat. But when they get to the house where Jesus is teaching, they find that it is so packed out in there, that they just can't get in - they are turned away at the door. Imagine their disappointment after having made such an effort to bring the man there only to find that they can't get to Jesus. Those friends must have really believed that if only they could have got to Jesus then he would have been able to do something for the man.

It's an extraordinary story. The friends are determined. Unstoppable. Talk about a 'can do' attitude. They go up onto the roof which they probably accessed by steps on the outside of the house and then they dismantle the roof until they have made a large hole. Then somehow they must have carried the man up the narrow steps to the roof. But can you imagine what it would have been like to have lowered the man down through the roof without tipping him off the mat. As you can see in the picture the friends are working together to support the weight of the man. I expect one of them was taking the lead and giving instructions, perhaps counting the man down as they gently let out the rope and ease him down, being careful not to drop him.

What these friends did was to very gently lower this man into the presence of the Lord. Jesus knew what that man needed. The friends brought him for healing, but in fact Jesus knew that the man needed forgiveness. He was first forgiven and then healed.

When we come here to worship together every week we are in fact coming into the presence of Jesus. Thankfully we don't have to take the roof off to be able to come to Jesus it is easier for us, but we do have to leave the households or units or places where we live. Some of us have to come in the lift or be brought by the staff. Some of us have to use a hoist or a wheelchair. We have to make a small effort to come. Also we help one another when we encourage each other to come and when we sit together and help one another in the service. The lovely thing is that when we arrive Jesus is already here waiting for us and not only that he knows what we really need.

Just have a think now... Why did you come to the service today? Is there something you really need from Jesus? Do you need healing or forgiveness like the man in the story? Do you need peace or strength or hope from Jesus? Would you like to pray for someone dear to you? All you have to do is ask him for what you need. He will hear your prayer. When we come to our prayers in a moment we will come to Jesus and pray to him for what we need.

Prayers

As we come to our time of prayer, let us remember that Jesus is here, waiting for us to come to him and he knows just what we need even before we ask him.

Lord Jesus we thank you that you are in this house. We come to you now and ask you for what we need.

In a moment of quiet whisper to Jesus and tell him what you need.....

We bring our loved ones to you Jesus. We pray that you would bless them and be close to them and give them what they need.

We pray that you will touch us with your healing and take away our pain. We pray that you would lift us up when we feel sad. We ask that you would give us your peace when we feel worried or afraid. Please give us your strength when we feel weak or tired. Please be always with us and close to us especially when we feel lonely.

Lord in your mercy....

We bring the staff, managers and volunteers and all who care for us to you Lord Jesus. We pray that you would bless them in their work and fill them with love and compassion.

Lord in your mercy....

We bring to Jesus all those who are suffering and who need healing. We pray Lord Jesus that you would touch them all with your healing and forgiveness.

Lord in your mercy...

The Lord's Prayer

Jesus' mother and brothers
We are God's family - Part I

Welcome and Introduction

Opening Response:

Leader:	Young and old Friends and strangers
All:	**We are God's family**

Leader:	Lost and bewildered Found and rejoicing
All:	**We are God's family**

Leader:	This morning, this day This night, for ever
All:	**We are God's family**

Hymn:	Thank you Lord for this fine day

Confession

Leader:	Lord forgive us
All:	**Lord forgive us and help us.**

Lord Jesus we come before you today just as we are with our strengths and weaknesses, our doubts and fears, our joys and sorrows.

For the times when we have closed ourselves to God and not loved him with all of our heart. Lord forgive us….

For the times when we have closed ourselves to one another and not loved one another fully. Lord forgive us…

May God our Father forgive us and help us to love him and our neighbours, that we might continue to grow together as a community of love and faith. **Amen**

Reading: Mark 3:31-35

Talk

Hymn: Lord of all hopefulness

Prayers
Leader: Lord in your mercy
All: **Hear our prayer**

Let us draw all these prayers together in the words of
The Lord's Prayer

All: **Our Father who art in Heaven……**

Hymn: He's got the whole world in his hands

Blessing:
                     May the Lord bless us and keep us
                     May the Lord make his face to shine upon us
                     and give us his peace. **Amen**

All: **The Grace.**

Talk

Just to put this little story into some sort of context. Jesus had been going through an extremely busy time in his ministry. Wherever he went he was followed by crowds of people all eager to hear his teaching and receive his healing. The Bible says that crowds even gathered in the house he was staying in so that he and his disciples didn't even have time to eat. His family hear about all this and they think he must have gone completely mad, so they come to see him to try and take charge of him. When they arrive, the place is absolutely packed, they can't get in, so they send a message to Jesus who is busy teaching. "Your mother and brothers are outside looking for you." Jesus' reply at first reading sounds a bit harsh, "Who are my mother and brothers?" "You here are my mother and brothers.

I did once see a film which I thought portrayed this scene very well, where Jesus receives the message and gets up to go to the door. As he makes his way he turns back into the room and says to everyone there, "Who are my mother and brothers – everyone who does God's will is my brother and sister and mother."

What did Jesus mean, "Everyone who does God's will is my brother, my sister and my mother?"

I think that what Jesus was saying was that although he had been brought up in a family, he did not belong only to them, and they could not possess him. He was saying that his family extended far beyond his own relatives. He was looking at the group of people gathered around him to listen to his teaching and was saying to them, "You are my family." Beyond the gathering in the house he was saying, 'Everyone who does the will of God is my family.' He had a sense of his own mission that he hadn't just come to the family he was born into, or even just to his own nation but that he had come for all people. The whole world.

Today, we are gathering together in this home and Jesus is here with us. As we worship and pray and share fellowship together, we are in fact being Jesus' family, the family of God and that means we are brothers and sisters to one another. As we think and pray for one another and for our loved ones and the staff and volunteers here in this home we are drawing them too into this family. As we extend our prayers for our world we are thinking of the whole human family to which we belong and we are drawing all of them into our time with God here now.

Prayers

Today as we pray together we are going to think about families.....

Heavenly Father we thank you for the sense of belonging and family that we experience here. Thank you for the support and care which we share with one another in this place. We thank you that we belong to you and that you recognise us as your family. Lord in your mercy.....

We thank you for all the staff and volunteers who care for us here and pray that you will bless them and their families, that you will give them your strength, your compassion and love.
Lord in your mercy....

We pray for all our loved ones, families, friends and neighbours. May they be blessed with your strength, patience and peace. May they know your presence and care for them.
Lord in your mercy......

We pray for all those known to us who are suffering in any way in body, mind or spirit. Please be close to them, may they know your comfort and care and your joy and hope to lift their spirits.
Lord in your mercy....

We pray for all those who suffer loneliness and isolation, for those who are homeless or who live alone and do not have the support of a loving family around them. May they be drawn into your loving family and know your care and comfort.
Lord in your mercy.....

We pray for the wider world wherever there is conflict, suffering and hardship we pray for peace.
Lord in your mercy.....

We are Gods family - Part II

Welcome and Introduction

Opening Response:

Leader:	Young and old
	Friends and strangers
All:	**We are God's family**

Leader:	Lost and bewildered
	Found and rejoicing
All:	**We are God's family**

Leader:	This morning, this day
	This night, forever
All:	**We are God's family**

Hymn:	How great thou art

Confession

Leader:	Lord forgive us
All:	**Lord forgive us and help us.**

Lord Jesus we come before you today just as we are with our strengths and weaknesses, our doubts and fears, our joys and sorrows.

For the times when we have closed ourselves to God and not loved him with all of our heart. Lord forgive us….

For the times when we have closed ourselves to one another and not loved one another fully. Lord forgive us…

May God our Father forgive us and help us to love him and our neighbours, that we might continue to grow together as a community of love and faith. **Amen**

Reading: Mark 3:31-35

Talk

Hymn: Thank you Jesus

Prayers
Leader: Lord in your mercy
All: **Hear our prayer**

Let us draw all these prayers together in the words of
The Lord's Prayer

All: **Our Father who art in Heaven……**

Hymn: He's got the whole world

Blessing:

                      May the Lord bless us and keep us
                      May the Lord make his face to shine upon us
                      and give us his peace. **Amen**

All: **The Grace**

Talk

Those of you who were here with us last week might remember that we had the same theme for our service – 'We are God's family', and the same reading. But just to recap. Jesus was going through a very busy time in his ministry. He was surrounded by crowds of people wherever he went and sometimes didn't even have time to eat. One day when he is teaching the people in a house, his mother and brothers come to see that he is alright and to make sure he is eating properly and getting enough rest. As he goes out to meet them he says something rather odd, "Who are my mother and brothers? Here are my mother and brothers. Whoever does the will of God is my brother and sister and mother."

Last week we thought about the fact that when we gather together in this home we are just like the early disciples gathered in that house and Jesus says to us you are my family. When we worship and pray together we are being the family of God. But there is more. Jesus said whoever does the will of God is my brother and sister and mother.

What did Jesus mean?
Whoever does the will of God is my brother, sister and mother?
And what is the will of God?
And how do we become a member of God's family?

Well the Bible says that it is God's will that we believe in Jesus, that Jesus is the Son of God the one that God sent into the world and that we trust him as our Saviour. The song we learnt today goes...

Thank you Lord for loving me.
You went to Calvary and there you died for me....so that we could come to know God as our father.
You rose up from the grave, to me knew life you gave....new life in him.

It is never too late to believe and trust in Jesus and to become a member of God's family. You can speak to us afterwards if you would like to know more about becoming part of God's family.

Let's sing thank you Jesus......

Prayers

Today as we pray together we thank God for sending his son Jesus to be our Saviour.

Heavenly Father we thank you that when Jesus came he showed us the way to become part of God's family and that as we believe and trust in him we come to know God as our Father and we experience a new life in Jesus.
Lord in your mercy....... hear our prayer.....

We thank you for all the staff and volunteers who care for us here and pray that you will bless them and their families, that you will give them your strength, your compassion and love.
Lord in your mercy....

We pray for all our loved ones, families, friends and neighbours. May they be blessed with your strength, patience and peace. May they know your presence and care for them.
Lord in your mercy......

We pray for all those known to us who are suffering or not very well. Please be close to them we pray, may they know your comfort and care and your joy and hope to lift their spirits.
Lord in your mercy....

We pray for all those who suffer loneliness and isolation, for those who are homeless or who live alone and do not have the support of a loving family around them. May they be drawn into your loving family and know your care and comfort.
Lord in your mercy.....

The precious pearl

Visual display: A pearl necklace

Welcome and Introduction

Opening Response:

Leader:	Round about us
	Here among us
All:	**God welcomes us with love**
Leader:	Good and faithful
	Strong in mercy
All:	**God welcomes us with love**
Leader:	Calling our names
	Bidding us welcome
All:	**God welcomes us with love**

Hymn: Praise my Soul

Confession:

Leader:	Lord forgive us
All:	**Lord forgive us and help us.**

Lord Jesus we come before you today just as we are with our strengths and weaknesses, our doubts and fears, our joys and sorrows.

For the times when we have closed ourselves to God and not loved him with all our heart. Lord forgive us….

For the times when we have closed ourselves to one another and not loved one another fully. Lord forgive us…

May God our Father forgive us and help us to love him and our neighbours that we might grow together as a community of love and faith. **Amen**

Reading: Matthew 13:44- 46

Talk

Hymn: Now thank we all our God

Prayers
Leader: Lord in your mercy
All: **Hear our prayer**

Let us draw all these prayers together in the words of
The Lord's Prayer

All: **Our Father who art in Heaven……**

Hymn: Give me joy in my heart

Blessing:

                    Fear not for I have redeemed you, I have
                    called you by name, you are mine. You are
                    precious and honoured in my sight and I love
                    you. May God bless us and keep us safe in the
                    palm of his hand. Amen

All: **The Grace**

Talk

Our reading today was one of Jesus' parables. Parables are little stories which Jesus often told to help people to understand what God is like. The story we heard today is about precious pearls.

I have brought some precious pearls to show you today – (show them around) Have any of you every worn some pearls like this?
These pearls belonged to my grandmother and they were a gift from my grandfather to her. She leant them to me when I got married, so I wore them on my wedding day with my wedding dress. Did any of you wear pearls when you got married? Then when my grandmother died about 13 years ago, she left me these pearls. As you can imagine, these pearls are precious to me, because they remind me of my grandmother and of my wedding day.

In his story, Jesus talks about a merchant who went around the world looking for precious pearls and when he found them, he sold everything he had –his home and all his belongings, everything, so that he could have this one precious pearl. It meant so much to him and he wanted it so much that he was prepared to give up everything else.

But if this is a story to tell us what God is like - what does it mean?
In this story, each one of us is like these precious pearls to God. We are so very precious to him that he was prepared to give up everything to have us for his own. When Jesus came to earth and was born as a baby in Bethlehem he gave up everything and he came here as one of us, so that he could tell us how much God loves us.

This is something for us to remember today, that each one of us is like a precious pearl to God. He loves us so much.

I want to finish by reading you a few verses from the book of Isaiah which read a bit like a love letter to us from God.

This is God speaking to us today…….
He says,
'Do not be afraid, for I have redeemed you
I have called you by name
You are mine
You are precious and honoured in my sight and I love you.'

Prayers

As we come to our time of prayer we remember that we are precious to God and he loves us.

Heavenly Father we thank you that we are together with you today. Please bless all the residents here in this care home. May they all know how much you love them. Lord in your mercy……

We thank you for all those who care for us, for the staff and managers and volunteers. Thank you for their dedication and please fill them with compassion and love. Lord in your mercy……

We pray for all our loved ones, families, friends and neighbours, please be close to them and bless them. Lord in your mercy….

We draw all these prayers together in the words of **The Lord's Prayer.**

Feeding the five thousand

Visual display: Basket of bread & fishes

Welcome and Introduction

Opening Response:

Leader:	The Lord is here among us
All:	**We give ourselves to him**

Leader:	The Lord is here to bless us
All:	**We give ourselves to him**

Leader:	The Lord makes us a gift to others
All:	**We give ourselves to him**

Hymn: Praise my soul

Let us confess our sin:

Leader:	Lord forgive us
All:	**Lord forgive us and help us.**

For the times we have forgotten to love you and give you thanks for all your goodness. Lord forgive us….

For the times we have been unkind or forgotten to love those around us.
Lord forgive us…..

Lord forgive us and help us to love you and our neighbours that we might grow together as a community of love and faith.

| Reading: | John 6:1-13 |

Talk

| **Hymn:** | Take my life |

Prayers
| Leader: | Lord in your mercy |
| **All:** | **Hear our prayer** |

Let us draw all these prayers together in the words of
The Lord's Prayer

| **All:** | **Our Father who art in Heaven……** |

| **Hymn:** | Now thank we all our God |

Blessing:

Now to him who is able to do immeasurably more than all we ask or imagine, according to his power that is at work within us, to him be glory forever, and may God bless us and keep us and hold us in the palm of his hand, today and every day. **Amen** *(Eph: 3:20)*

| **All:** | **The Grace** |

Talk

Well we have just heard the story of an extraordinary miracle. By this time in his ministry Jesus had become quite a celebrity. He had a huge following of people that were really interested in him because they had heard about his healing miracles and so wherever he went he was surrounded by people. He tended to go out into countryside places or into the hills where large crowds could gather to listen to his teaching. I have actually been to the place where the feeding of the 5000 was meant to have happened. Have any of you been to the Mount of the Beatitudes? It is a grassy meadow right next to Lake Galilee and is a natural bowl shape a bit like an amphitheatre. The acoustics are amazing, so that we could sit at the top and hear what people were saying right down at the bottom. It was easy for me to imagine 5000 people there sitting having a picnic together. We know the story, this crowd of people had been out there listening to Jesus all day, it was getting late and was time for everyone to go home for dinner. But of course, they were miles from anywhere. The disciples wanted Jesus to send everyone home, but Jesus had other ideas. He wanted them all to stay and eat together and he was planning something special. I think he must have been teasing the disciples when he tells them that it's their job to feed everyone. I can imagine the disciples getting a bit exasperated with him, when they say, "Well all there is are 5 loaves and 2 fish, but what good is that?"

But what happens next is really quite amazing. Jesus says, "Ask everyone to sit down in smaller groups" Then he takes the bread and fishes in his hands, blesses the food and gives thanks a bit like we do when we say grace before a meal and then he begins to distribute it to his disciples to go around serving everyone. We don't quite know what did happen, but it seems that as they distribute the food it is multiplied and somehow becomes more and more, so that everyone is fed and there are some leftovers. It is a wonderful story that we are still telling today 2000 years later.

But what does it mean? Is there a message for us today? Well yes there is. The message is, that Jesus was able to take a little offering – some little boy's picnic tea and when he took it and blessed it somehow it became something so much more, in fact it was enough to feed a great crowd of people. The same is true for us today. We may look at ourselves and think "Well I haven't got much to give, I'm not of much use these days, there's not much I can do now." But if we do what that little boy did and put ourselves into the hands of Jesus, he will take us and bless us, just like he did the bread and fishes and make us a special blessing to others. If we give over our little selves, our little lives to Jesus, he is able to transform us into something much more than we could ever imagine.

Prayers

As we come to our time of prayer, in a few moments quiet, try to imagine the scene – the big crowd of people all gathered to listen to Jesus, the disciples scratching their heads and wondering how on earth they are going to feed everybody and the little boy stepping forward with his little offering of 5 loaves and 2 fish.

I am going to pray a prayer offering ourselves and our little lives to Jesus, you can pray this prayer in your own heart if you want to.

Lord Jesus I offer to you today the small gift of myself. It may not be much, but I ask that you bless me today and make me a blessing to others. Please take the little I am giving you and make it into something much bigger, so that all those around me may know how much you love them. Amen.

> Take my love; my Lord I pour
> At thy feet its treasure store
> Take myself and I will be
> Ever, only, all for thee

The wedding at Cana

Visual display: Wedding photographs – residents', leader's

Welcome and Introduction

Opening responses:

Leader:	In my living and in my loving
All:	**You have blessed me**

Leader:	In my tears and in my laughter
All:	**You have blessed me**

Leader:	In my sisters and in my brothers
All:	**You have blessed me**

Leader:	With everything that's in me
All:	**give you thanks**

Hymn:	The King of love

Confession
Leader:	Lord forgive us
All:	**Lord forgive us and help us.**

Lord Jesus we come before you today just as we are with our strengths and weaknesses, our doubts and fears, our joys and sorrows.

For the times when we have closed ourselves to God and not loved him with all our heart. Lord forgive us....

For the times when we have closed ourselves to one another and not loved one another fully. Lord forgive us...

May God our Father forgive us and help us to love him and our neighbours here that we might continue to grow together as a community of love and faith. **Amen**

259

Reading:	John 2: 1-11

Talk

Hymn: Love divine

Prayers:
Leader: Lord in your mercy
All: **Hear our prayer**

Let us draw all these prayers together in the words of
The Lord's Prayer

All: **Our Father who art in Heaven……**

Hymn: Give me joy in my heart

Blessing

May the Lord bless us and keep us.
May the Lord make his face to shine upon us
and be gracious to us.
May the Lord lift up the light of his
countenance on us and give us his peace.
Amen

All: **The Grace**

Talk

I particularly like this story because we see Jesus in a very human situation, attending a wedding party with his mother and his friends.

Usually at weddings there is something that doesn't quite go to plan. If you think back to your own weddings I expect you can think of something that went wrong. (Invite residents to share some stories and/ or share your own story) Well at this wedding there was an embarrassing situation. The party was in full swing and the wine had run out. We don't know if the couple themselves were aware of what had happened, but it is Jesus' mother Mary who realises and has a quiet word with Jesus.

When Jesus is told about the wine, first of all he says, "Why are you telling me, what am I supposed to do about it?" But Mary knew something. She knew that he would be able to help, and I think she intuitively knew that he would help and so she has a quiet word with the servants, "Just do whatever he tells you to do."

We know the story. Jesus tells the servants to fill up the stone water jars with water – holding 20-30 gallons and then to pour it out and serve it to the master of the banquet and we know that it wasn't just cheap plonk because he comments on it being the finest of wine. And the party carries on in full swing probably for several days as was the Middle Eastern tradition.

It's a lovely story, but what does it say to us here today? It tells us that just as Jesus was perfectly at home sharing in the joy and celebration of his friends at their wedding, he is also perfectly at home with us here. In this home I know that you sometimes have parties and celebrations and there is often lots of fun and laughter. I believe that Jesus is with us in the midst of all these joyful times. But also, this story tells us of the extravagant love of God. Jesus turned water into wine. Not just a couple of bottles but more than 100 gallons of wine. What was he thinking of?! That really says something about God doesn't it? That he loves us with an extravagant, abundant, everlasting sort of love, a love that bubbles up and keeps overflowing, running over. Loads and loads of love. Sometimes we have been especially aware of that love when we have met together here and shared in worship together and experienced the joy of singing together.

Hymn   Love divine

Let's sing this song joyfully and give thanks God's great love for us.

Prayers

As we come to our time of prayer let us give thanks for God's abundant love and goodness which we experience in our life together here.

Lord Jesus, we thank you that you have made your home with us here and that you share in all that we go through here. Thank you for all the joy and laughter the fun and celebration that is part of our life together. Lord in your mercy....

We thank you for all the love that we give and receive from one another. Especially we thank you for the loving care we receive from the care staff and volunteers. We pray that you will bless them and their families. Lord in your mercy...

We pray for all those known to us who are suffering in anyway and especially for members of our community currently in hospital. Please bring them your comfort, peace and healing. Lord in your mercy....

Let us draw all these prayers together in the words of **The Lord's Prayer.**

Who do you say I am?

Pictures:	Images of Jesus - Jesus blesses the children, Jesus on the cross, On the road to Emmaus. The Benedictine Nuns of Turvey Abbey.

Welcome and Introduction

Opening Response:

Leader:	Faithful and wise
All:	**God is our friend**

Leader:	Honest and true
All:	**God is our friend**

Leader:	Keeper of promises
All:	**God is our friend**

Hymn:	Lord of all hopefulness

Confession:

Leader:	Lord forgive us
All:	**Lord forgive us and help us.**

Lord Jesus we come before you today just as we are with our strengths and weaknesses, our doubts and fears, our joys and sorrows.

For the times when we have closed ourselves to God and not loved him with all of our heart. Lord forgive us….

For the times when we have closed ourselves to one another and not loved one another fully. Lord forgive us…

May God our Father forgive us and help us to love him and our neighbours that we might grow together as a community of love and faith. **Amen**

Reading:	Matthew 16:13-17

Talk

Hymn	How sweet the name of Jesus

Prayers
Leader:	Lord in your mercy
All:	**Hear our prayer**

Let us draw all these prayers together in the words of
The Lord's Prayer

All:	**Our Father who art in Heaven……**

Hymn:	Lord Jesus Christ (Living Lord)

Blessing:	To him who is able to keep us from falling and to present us before his glorious presence without fault and with great joy. To the only God our Saviour be glory, majesty, power and authority through Jesus Christ our Lord. **Amen**

All:	**The Grace**

Talk

We know that during Jesus' public ministry he spent a lot of time on the road with his disciples walking from village to village. I imagine that while they were walking along together they had all sorts of conversations. Today we read of one of these conversations. Jesus asks his disciples, "What are people saying about me? Who do they think I am?" The disciples would have often mingled in the crowds and heard people talking about him, so they tell Jesus, "Well people think you are one of the prophets, perhaps John the Baptist or Elijah or Jeremiah."

I wonder, how do you think we would answer that question today?

I think perhaps some people would say that Jesus was a prophet, a teacher, a good, wise man. Many people today think of Jesus as a historical figure, a baby on a Christmas card or someone in a painting or a stained-glass window. Some people today really know nothing about him.

And then Jesus asks them very directly, "What about you, who do you think I am?"

Peter had come to realise that Jesus was no ordinary man, not just a prophet or a teacher but that he was the Christ, the Son of the Living God, the one they had all been waiting for.

I wonder if Jesus were to ask us this question, "What about you, who do you think I am?" What would we say? Would any of you like to answer that question now?

Perhaps you would like to think about who Jesus is for you. Perhaps your relationship with him has changed over the years and now you have a different understanding of him from when you were young.

When I was a child I was brought up to believe that Jesus was my friend that he was close to me a bit like an older brother or member of the family. My prayers were very simple, telling him about my day, asking him to help me and to bless the people I loved.

As a young person I came to know and understand that Jesus was my Saviour. I realised that he had suffered on the cross for me so that all that was wrong in my life could be forgiven and I could come close to God and know him as my Father. I came to appreciate how much he loved me.

But as I grew up I went through all the usual ups and downs of life, the joys and sorrows, grief, disappointments and losses and so on. I came to understand Jesus as his name Emmanuel that means God is with us. I realised that in the midst of whatever was happening he was with me and that I could pray for guidance and strength. I could experience the peace of knowing that he would never leave me alone.

Prayers

Lord Jesus as we come to you now in prayer we thank you for all you mean to each one of us All of us have a different story to tell of how we have come to know you and how you have been with us throughout our lives. Thank you that you are the Christ, the son of the living God, alive and with us now. Lord in your mercy……

We pray for all those with whom we share our lives here. We pray that you would help us to grow into a community of love and faith, that we may serve one another with care and compassion Lord in your mercy….

We pray for all those who care for us here, for the staff and volunteers. Please bless them and their families, please fill them with your tender love and gentleness. Lord in your mercy…

We pray for all those known to us who are suffering in anyway in body, mind or spirit. Especially we pray for all those in hospital and in prison, for those who are homeless and poor, for those who are lonely and have no one to pray for them. Lord in your mercy….

We pray for your peace and healing to come to all the troubled places of our world, where there is war, famine and natural disaster. Lord in your mercy……

Let us draw all these prayers together in the words of **The Lord's Prayer**.

Mary and Martha

Picture: Mary and Martha by The Benedictine Nuns
of Turvey Abbey

Welcome and Introduction

Opening Response:

Leader: The Lord is here
All: **We welcome him into our home**

Leader: The Lord is here
All: **We welcome him here among us**

Leader: The Lord is here
All: **We welcome him into our hearts**

Hymn: Dear Lord and Father

Confession:

Leader: Lord forgive us
All: **Lord forgive us and help us.**

Lord Jesus we come before you today just as we are with our strengths and weaknesses, our doubts and fears, our joys and sorrows.

For the times when we have closed ourselves to God and not loved him with all of our heart. Lord forgive us....

For the times when we have closed ourselves to one another and not loved one another fully. Lord forgive us...

May God our Father forgive us and help us to love him and our neighbours that we might grow together as a community of love and faith. **Amen**

Reading: Luke 10: 38-42

Talk

Hymn: Blessed Assurance

Prayers
Leader: Lord in your mercy
All: **Hear our prayer**

Let us draw all these prayers together in the words of
The Lord's Prayer

All: **Our Father who art in Heaven……**

Hymn: Come down O love divine

Blessing:

        The gentle peace of God,
flows freely, encircles fully,
refreshes gently, comforts warmly,
reassures softly, forgives easily,
fulfils entirely. May this gentle peace of God be
with you, and all whom you love now and
always. **Amen.**

All: **The Grace**

Talk

Today we have this story of Jesus coming to visit two very dear friends, Martha and Mary, who were sisters. This story gives us an insight into two very different personalities, and two very different ways of welcoming Jesus. Martha welcomes Jesus by being very busy with all sorts of preparations. We can imagine her cleaning the house and wanting to have everything in order. We can imagine her laying a nice table and preparing a delicious meal. She wants to have everything just right for him. Mary in contrast welcomes Jesus by sitting down amongst the disciples, by listening to him and giving him her full attention. Martha feels resentful that she has been left to do all the work and wants Jesus to tell Mary off for sitting there when there is work to be done. But Jesus refuses to do this and instead commends Mary for giving him her attention.

This is one of those stories that most people can identify with, and often people think that Jesus is a bit hard on Martha because after all if she had not done the work no one would have had anything to eat that day!

My feeling about this story is that Jesus was not telling Martha off for serving, but that he was asking her to keep things simple and to not be worried about the details. He wanted her to work out her priorities so that she had time to relax and be with him too.

I think too that this story can be about different times in our lives. Many of you have told me something of the story of your lives and I know that you have been through periods in life when you have worked very hard and had very little time for yourselves. Many of you have had demanding jobs and family lives and periods where you have been very busy caring for others or serving in your local communities. Some of you have been active members of your churches. You have shown your love for God through active service rather like Martha.

But now you have come to a different stage in life where the work is done, the children and grandchildren have been brought up. It may be now that you are able to identify yourselves more with Mary who was commended by Jesus for just being with him, taking time to relax with him, to listen to him, to share with him. Mary helped Jesus to feel very welcome in their home because she gave time to just be with him, to be attentive to him. What she did was really valued by Jesus. He even said she had chosen the better way.

As we gather together each week, we come to meet with Jesus, to sit at his feet, to listen to him, to just be with him. He feels welcome in our home here and enjoys resting, relaxing with us here. There are times too when you will find yourselves enjoying a bit of peace and quiet in your own room and Jesus is with you there enjoying being at home with you.

Prayers

Just as Jesus came to the home of Mary and Martha in Bethany, he comes to our home here Let us come close to him now as we pray together. Let us pray.

Lord Jesus we come now to sit at your feet to bring you ourselves, our lives our concerns. Thank you that you are always with us in all we go through in life, you know our needs and you do hear our prayers. Lord in your mercy……

We pray for all those with whom we share our lives here. We pray that you would help us to grow into a community of love and faith, that we may serve one another with care and compassion Lord in your mercy….

We pray for all those who care for us here. Please bless them and their families, please fill them with your tender love and gentleness. Lord in your mercy…

We pray for all those known to us who are suffering in anyway in body, mind or spirit. Especially we pray for all those in hospital and in prison, for those who are homeless and poor, for those who are lonely and have no one to pray for them. Lord in your mercy….

We pray for your peace and healing to come to all the troubled places of our world, where there is war, famine and natural disaster. Lord in your mercy……

Let us draw all these prayers together in the words of **the Lord's Prayer.**

Be thankful

Welcome and Introduction

Let the peace of Christ rule in your hearts, since as members of one body you were called to peace. And be thankful…And whatever you do whether in word or deed, do it all in the name of the Lord Jesus giving thanks to God the Father through him. (Col 3:15,17)

Opening response:

Leader: Young and old
Friends and strangers

All: **God welcomes us**

Leader: Lost and bewildered
Found and rejoicing

All: **God welcomes us**

Leader: This morning, this day
This night, for ever

All: **God welcomes us**

Hymn: All things bright and beautiful

Confession
Leader: Lord forgive us
All: **Lord forgive us and help us.**

Lord Jesus we come before you today just as we are with our strengths and weaknesses, our doubts and fears, our joys and sorrows.

For the times when we have closed ourselves to God and not loved him with all our heart. Lord forgive us….

For the times when we have closed ourselves to one another and not loved one another fully. Lord forgive us…

May God our Father forgive us and help us to love him and our neighbours here, that we might continue to grow together as a community of love and faith. **Amen**

Reading:	Luke 17: 11-19

Talk

Hymn: Now thank we all our God

Prayers:
Leader: Lord in your mercy
All: **Hear our prayer**

Let us draw all these prayers together in the words of
The Lord's Prayer

All: **Our Father who art in Heaven……**

Hymn: Give me joy in my heart

Blessing from
Psalm 67:

> May God be gracious to us and bless us
> May the Lord make his face to shine upon us
> May the peoples praise you O God
> May the nations be glad and sing for joy
> Then the land will yield its harvest and God our
> God will bless us. **Amen**

All: **The Grace**

Talk

Today we are thinking about the importance of saying thank you and this is something that I think that we can really learn from your generation. Can you remember being told as children to mind your Ps and Qs? There was a certain level of politeness and respect that perhaps we have lost a little bit today.

This is a story about 10 lepers.
Explain about leprosy

There are various stories about Jesus touching lepers and making them well. He didn't seem to have any fear of catching leprosy. In this case he just tells them to go and see a priest and they find that they are healed before they even get there. We perhaps don't quite realise the enormity of what has happened. Jesus not only made them well, but in effect he had given them back their lives. They could go back to their families, hold their children, do a normal job, be part of the community again, no longer isolated and kept separate with people running away from them for fear of catching leprosy. It must have been wonderful. I think if that had happened to me I would have been absolutely overflowing with thankfulness. But if you listened to the story out of the ten lepers who were healed only one of them came back to say thank you to God.

I wonder why that was?
Perhaps it was that they were so overjoyed they just forgot. All they could think of was going home and getting on with their lives.
Perhaps they didn't realise that it was God who had healed them, or they didn't believe in God and so didn't think to thank him.

Jesus in fact expresses surprise that only one has come back and says "Where are the other nine were not all ten healed?"

So why is it important to say thank you to God for all he has given to us?
There is an expression I like – cultivate an attitude of gratitude.

First of all, it is about opening our eyes to see all the blessings of our lives and then simply saying thank you. When we do this regularly even daily it makes us better people. We feel happier and our thankfulness and happiness is contagious, it spreads to those who we live with.
Also, its easy to do – just like the song we sang earlier…

Thank you, Lord, for this fine day
Thank you, Lord, for all those who care for us

Thank you, Lord, for food to eat
Thank you, Lord, for friends and family

This attitude of gratitude can spread to the staff as well. Its noticing all that the carers do for us and remembering to say thank you.

Thank you for helping me get dressed
Thank you for tidying my bedroom
Thank you for listening to me when I'm feeling down.

Thank you for serving my meal
Thank you for putting away my laundry

We are going to sing a hymn of thankfulness now, and as we sing it I encourage all of us to think about all the blessings of our lives that we would like to say thank you for.

Hymn: Now thank we all our God

Prayers

As we come to our time of prayer we give thanks for all God's blessings.

Heavenly Father we thank you for all you give to us every day. We thank you for our comfortable home, where we are safe and well and for our food.

We thank you for the staff who care for our needs. Thank you for their kindness and compassion, their patience and their tender loving care.

We thank you for all our friends and relatives who come to visit us and for all those who think about us and pray for us.

We thank you that we can meet together every week to worship you together.

Especially we thank you that you are always with us and that you love us.

Lord in your mercy.... Hear our prayer.

Called by name

Welcome and Introduction

"Speak Lord for your servant is listening" (1 Sam 3:10)

Opening response:

Leader:	The Lord is here among us
All:	**He calls us by name**

Leader:	The Lord loves us
All:	**He calls us by name**

Leader:	The Lord is always with us
All:	**He calls us by name**

Hymn:	Holy, holy, holy

Confession

Leader:	Lord forgive us
All:	**Lord forgive us and help us.**

Lord Jesus we come before you today just as we are with our strengths and weaknesses, our doubts and fears, our joys and sorrows.

For the times when we have closed ourselves to God and not loved him with all our heart. Lord forgive us….

For the times when we have closed ourselves to one another and not loved one another fully. Lord forgive us…

May God our Father forgive us and help us to love him and our neighbours here, that we might continue to grow together as a community of love and faith. **Amen**

Reading: 1 Samuel 3:2-10

Talk

Hymn: Great is thy faithfulness

Prayers:
Leader: Lord in your mercy
All: **Hear our prayer**

Let us draw all these prayers together in the words of
The Lord's Prayer

All: **Our Father who art in Heaven......**

Hymn: He's got the whole world in his hands

Blessing:

                  God says to us.....
                  Fear not for I have redeemed you
                  I have called you by name
                  You are mine
                  You are precious and honoured in my sight
                  and I love you. (Is 43)

                  May God bless us and keep us
                  and hold us in the palm of his hand

All: **The Grace**

Introduction to the reading

The story we are about to listen to is about a young boy called Samuel. His mother Hannah had been unable to have children and she was very sad about it. One day she and her family are in Jerusalem. She goes on her own to the temple and prays to God to be able to have a child. She makes a promise to God that if he hears her prayer and gives her a child, she will give the child back into the Lord's service. This is what happens. The Lord answers her prayer, she gives birth to Samuel and when he is only five years old, she takes him to the temple and hands him over to Eli a very elderly priest to be his servant. One night when Eli and Samuel have both gone to bed an extraordinary thing happens.....

Reading: 1 Sam 3:2-10

Talk

This is a lovely story of the little boy Samuel who is serving in the Temple. He goes to bed one night and is woken by a voice calling his name, Samuel! Samuel! Of course, he thinks it is Eli calling for him, so he jumps out of bed and runs to Eli, but Eli says, "No I didn't call you, go back to bed."

As we have heard this happens three times. Samuel hears someone calling his name, Samuel! Samuel!
In the end Eli realises that it must be the Lord calling to Samuel, so he tells him, "Go back to bed and if you hear the voice again, then reply, "Speak Lord for your servant is listening."

Later when he grows us, Samuel becomes a prophet. He listens to God speaking to him and then gives God's messages to the people.

Perhaps some of you can relate to this story, you may have become aware of God when you were very young. You may have heard about him when you went to Sunday School or to church or in your own families. I do believe that God calls to us throughout our lives and that he knows us by name. Just like he called to Samuel, he calls to each one of us too.

If we could hear the voice of God calling to us today, I wonder what we would hear him say?
I think we would hear him say something like this......
'Your name'..... you are my child, I know you by name, you are precious to me and I love you.

Prayers:

As we come to our time of prayer, let us give thanks that we are God's children and that he knows each one of us by name.

Heavenly Father, thank you that you know each one of us by name, that we are your precious children, and you love us, and are always with us. Lord in your mercy.....

We thank you for all the staff and volunteers who care for us. Please bless them and their families and help them to do their work with tenderness and compassion. Lord in your mercy.....

We pray for all our loved ones, our families, friends and neighbours, please take care of them and be close to them. Lord in your mercy....

We pray for all those known to us who are suffering in any way in body, mind or spirit, please bring them your strength, peace, comfort and healing. Lord in your mercy....

The Lord's Prayer

Holding onto the promises of God

Welcome and Introduction

Opening Responses:

Leader:	Round about us Here among us
All:	**God of promise and love**

Leader:	Good and faithful Strong in mercy
All:	**God of promise and love**

Leader:	Calling our names Bidding us welcome
All:	**God of promise and love**

Hymn:	Praise to the Lord, the Almighty the king of creation

Confession:

Loving God,
We have sinned against you in what we have thought, said and done. We have not always loved you with our whole heart; we have not always loved our neighbours as ourselves.
We are truly sorry and turn away from what is wrong. Forgive us for the sake of your son, Jesus Christ our Lord. **Amen.**

Christ Jesus came into the world to save sinners. This is his gracious word to us: 'Your sins are forgiven.' **Amen**

Reading: Genesis 15: 1-12, 17,18

Talk:

Hymn: Thy hand O God has guided

Prayers:
Leader: Lord in your mercy
All: **Hear our prayer**

Let us draw all these prayers together in the words of
The Lord's Prayer

All: **Our Father who art in Heaven…**

Hymn: Great is thy faithfulness

Blessing:

May the Lord bless us and make us a blessing
May the Lord make his face to shine upon us
and be gracious to us. May the Lord lift up the
light of his countenance upon us and give us his
peace. **Amen**

All: **The Grace**

Talk

The reading is the story of Abram who became known as Abraham.

Abraham is a wonderful example of a person who was faithful and trusted in God in older age. He was already an older man when God came to him and called him to leave his home and go to the land, God would show him. God asked him to leave his home, his land, his community, to leave everything behind and simply to go where God led him and that was it, there was no explanation. But at the same time God made some promises to Abraham.

This was the promise and blessing that God gave him:

'I will make you into a great nation, and I will bless you;
I will make your name great, and you will be a blessing.
I will bless those who bless you, and whoever curses you I will curse;
And all peoples on earth will be blessed through you.'

So, in effect God was promising to:
Give Abraham children who would one day become a great nation
Give Abraham a land
Make Abraham a blessing to all people, the whole earth.
(Gen 12: 2-3)

Abram, is obedient to God, he leaves his home and sets off not knowing where he will end up. He lives among strangers- not all of them friendly and he holds on to the promise of God. He waits and waits, and nothing appears to be happening – his wife still hasn't been able to have children. In fact she has gone past the age when women can have children.

And then we come to the reading we heard today where Abram says to God, "I know about your promise to me Lord, but still you have given me no children."

God takes him outside and shows him the night sky and says to him "Look up at the stars, count them if you can, your offspring will be as numerous as the stars in the sky." The Bible says that even though there was no evidence, no sign this would happen, Abram believed God.

As we know, Abram lived his later life well, holding onto God's promises and believing in him. He became fruitful in his old age and saw the beginnings of God's promise fulfilled when his wife Sarah gave birth to Isaac.

So, I wonder what this story is saying to us today?

Well, I think that some of you here have experienced something similar to Abram. You may perhaps have not thought of it like this before but those of you who are residents here like Abram have all been called by God to leave your home. You have had to let go of many of your possessions and leave behind your communities like he did. I know that it must have been hard and perhaps it all felt uncertain, you didn't know really what it would be like and perhaps when you first came it did feel rather strange living with people you didn't know and being cared for by people you didn't know. But just as God made some promises to Abram when he left everything behind, God has made some promises to us too.

What are those promises? Just listen to them:

God loves you. God is here with you. God has not abandoned you. God will never leave you nor forsake you. God will never forget you. God knows you by name, you are precious to him.

Not only that, God has not called you to leave your home for nothing, for no reason. He has a purpose for you being here. God's promise to Abram was that he would be a blessing to all people and to the whole earth. God's purpose for you here as this little Christian fellowship is that you would be a blessing to the whole of this place where you live, to the other residents and to the staff. You are here for a reason – to pray. To pray and to hold onto the promises of God. Just listen to them again:

God loves *this care home*. God is here with you. God has not abandoned. God will never leave you nor forsake you. God will never forget you. God knows everyone here by name, you are precious to him. When we come to our prayers in a moment, I would like to lead us in prayer especially for *this care home* and for all of you here.

281

Prayers

As we come now to our time of prayer, let us remember that God is with us here.
Heavenly Father, we thank you for leading and guiding us and caring for us throughout the past 10 years. Thank you for your promises to us that you are always with us, that you know us by name, and you love us.

We pray for all those who care for us here. We pray that you would fill them with patience and compassion and make them gentle and kind. We pray that you would give them your strength and fill them with joy in their work. Please bless them and their families.
Lord in your mercy..... **hear our prayer**

We pray for the managers and for all those in positions of responsibility and leadership in the home that you would give them your wisdom and direct them in the right path.
Lord in your mercy.... **Hear our prayer**

We pray for all our loved ones, families, friends and neighbours that you would be close to them all and bless them.
Especially we pray for.......
Lord in your mercy.....**Hear our prayer**

Let us draw all these prayers together in the words of **The Lord's Prayer**

The widow's offering

Picture: The widow's mite by The Benedictine Nuns
of Turvey Abbey

Welcome and Introduction

Opening Responses:

Leader: God of the past
God of our memories

All: **We give ourselves to you**

Leader: God of the future
God of our dreams

All: **We give ourselves to you**

Leader: God of the present
God of our salvation

All: **We give ourselves to you**

Hymn: Praise my soul

Confession:

Loving God,
We have sinned against you in what we have thought, said and done. We have not always loved you with our whole heart; we have not always loved our neighbours as ourselves.
We are truly sorry and turn away from what is wrong. Forgive us for the sake of your son, Jesus Christ our Lord. **Amen.**

Christ Jesus came into the world to save sinners. This is his gracious word to us: 'Your sins are forgiven.' **Amen**

Reading: Luke 21: 1- 4

Talk:

Hymn: Father we adore you
               Jesus we adore you
               Spirit we adore you

Prayers:
Leader: Lord in your mercy
All: **Hear our prayer**

Let us draw all these prayers together in the words of
The Lord's Prayer

All: **Our Father who art in Heaven…**

Hymn: Take my life and let it be

Blessing:

               May the Lord bless us and make us a blessing
               May the Lord make his face to shine upon us
               and be gracious to us. May the Lord lift up the
               light of his countenance upon us and give us his
               peace. **Amen**

All: **The Grace**

Talk

We have heard a very short reading about a time when Jesus was sitting in the temple courts in Jerusalem. Just before this, Jesus had been talking with some chief priests and teachers of the law. They were religious leaders and they had come to grill Jesus about various points of religious law. In fact they were trying corner him with their arguments and catch him out and they were looking for a reason to arrest him because they hated him and wanted to get rid of him. At the end of it Jesus says to his disciples,

"Beware of the teachers of the law. They like to walk around in flowing robes and love to be greeted in the market places and have the important seats in the synagogues and the places of honour at banquets. They devour widow's houses and for a show make lengthy prayers."

This picture shows these types of people- we can see these men with their rather proud faces coming along to the offering boxes with their big money bags to show how rich they are and looking around to see who is watching as they put handfuls of money in the offering. But then Jesus notices this older lady who is a poor widow. Her husband has died, she is too old to work and she is really struggling to make ends meet. She quietly comes to the offering box and puts in all she has - two pennies. It may have been enough to buy a bottle of milk or a loaf of bread or to put in the meter to heat her home for a little while. Jesus knows something about her circumstances and he makes a comparison between her and the men. He says, these men are all show, they appear to be giving a lot to the temple treasury but really it is very little because they are very rich. But this woman who has so little has given all she has.

I have sometimes wondered about this woman - we don't even know her name, but what she did has been recorded and here we are telling her story 2,000 years later. I wonder why she did give all she had? I think that she must have felt tremendous gratitude to God for all he had done for her and this sense of gratitude made her generous. Also she must have really trusted that God would provide for her needs because she went away with nothing just believing that he would be there for her. Finally she must have believed that her 2 pennies could make a difference, and could do some good.

So what does this story say to us today? Well, I think it tells us that God knows what is going on on the inside of us, in our hearts. It does not matter to God how rich or poor we are, what he really wants is for us to be like the widow in the story and to give him all that we are. We might feel a bit like this woman and say to ourselves, "What can I give to God? What difference can I make?" But actually a little prayer offering ourselves to God at the beginning of each day can make a big difference to how the day goes. If we invite God to come and fill our day and our life, extraordinary things can happen and it is often the little things which make all the difference. A smile, a kind greeting or a word of encouragement or thanks to those you live with and to the carers can really make everyone feel better. We all have our struggles and for many of us life can be hard. But God can take the little offerings of ourselves and really make a difference through us.

In a moment when we come to our time of prayer I am going to pray a prayer of offering ourselves to God and if you would like to do that then please pray it quietly in your own hearts and then at the end of the service we will give you a little card with this prayer on and if you want to you could pray this prayer each morning when you wake up and then wait and see what God will do with your little offering of yourself.

Prayer

Lord Jesus, I offer myself to you today. I pray that you would fill me with your love and keep me close to you each moment of this day. Help me to share your love with all those I meet today. Help me to speak kindly and gently to all those I live with and to all those who care for me. May your joy and peace flow through me today into this home. Lord please bless me and make me a blessing. In your name, Amen

The unmerciful servant

Welcome and Introduction

Opening Responses:
Leader: God of the past
                 God of our memories
All: **God of forgiveness and love**

Leader: God of the future
                 God of our dreams
All: **God of forgiveness and love**

Leader: God of the present
                 God of our salvation
All: **God of forgiveness and love**

Hymn: Amazing grace

Confession:

Loving God,
We have sinned against you in what we have thought, said and done. We have not always loved you with our whole heart; we have not always loved our neighbours as ourselves.
We are truly sorry and turn away from what is wrong. Forgive us for the sake of your son, Jesus Christ our Lord. **Amen.**

Christ Jesus came into the world to save sinners. This is his gracious word to us: 'Your sins are forgiven.' **Amen**

Reading: Matthew 18: 21-35

Talk:

Hymn: God forgave my sin (Freely, freely)

Prayers:
Leader: Lord in your mercy
All: **Hear our prayer**

Let us draw all these prayers together in the words of
The Lord's Prayer

All: **Our Father who art in Heaven…**

Hymn: When I survey the wondrous cross

Blessing:
            May the Lord bless us and make us a blessing
            May the Lord make his face to shine upon us
            and be gracious to us. May the Lord lift up the
            light of his countenance upon us and give us his
            peace. **Amen**

All: **The Grace**

Dramatic Reading: The Parable of the Unmerciful Servant
Matthew 18: 21-35

Narrator: Then Peter came to Jesus and asked,

Peter: "Lord, how many times shall I forgive my brother or sister who sins against me? Up to seven times?"

Jesus: "I tell you, not seven times, but seventy-seven times."
'Therefore, the kingdom of heaven is like a king who wanted to settle accounts with his servants. As he began the settlement, a man who owed him ten thousand bags of gold was brought to him. Since he was not able to pay, the master ordered that he and his wife and his children and all that he had be sold to repay the debt.'

Servant: (falls to his knees and begs) "Be patient with me and I will pay back everything."

Jesus: 'The servant's master took pity on him, cancelled the debt and let him go. But when that servant went out, he found one of his fellow servants who owed him a hundred silver coins.

Servant (grabbing the man and choking him) "Pay back what you owe me!"

Fellow servant (falling to the ground and begging) "Be patient with me, and I will pay it back."

Jesus: 'But he refused. Instead, he went off and had the man thrown into prison until he could pay the debt. When the other servants saw what had happened, they were outraged and went and told their master everything that had happened. Then the master called the servant in.'

Master: "You wicked servant, I cancelled all that debt of yours because you begged me to. Shouldn't you have had mercy on your fellow servant just as I had on you?"

Jesus: 'In anger his master handed him over to the jailers to be tortured, until he should pay back all he owed.'
"This is how my heavenly Father will treat each of you unless you forgive your brother or sister from your heart."

Talk

The reading we have just heard (seen acted) begins with a question. Peter asks Jesus, "How many times shall I forgive my brother when he sins against me? Seven times?" Jesus replies, "Not seven times but seventy-seven times." Some versions of the Bible even say seventy times seven times which would be 490 times!

It is human nature for us to sin against one another in our thoughts, in our words and in our actions. We might think that we haven't really done very much wrong, but the reality is that most of us do have bad thoughts about others, we do sometimes say hurtful things about others or gossip behind their backs. We have all been hurt by the words and actions of others too. In this reading Jesus is saying that the only way to deal with these sins is to keep forgiving on and on. If we can't forgive and we build up a record of wrongs against someone, then anger and bitterness will build up inside us and feel like heavy rocks in our hearts. Our hearts will become hard and we will find it hard to love and to give generously. In the end un-forgiveness really hurts us.

Jesus then goes on to tell a story to help us to understand what forgiveness is. It is about a servant who owes a huge debt, so huge he will never be able to pay it back. The master in the story wants to sell him and his family into slavery to repay the debt but the servant begs him to have mercy. The master is kind and generous and completely cancels the debt. All of us human beings are like this servant. The debt we can't pay back is the debt of our sin. This is everything we have done wrong throughout the whole of our lives. The master in the story is God. He has cancelled our debt and the way he did it was to send Jesus to die on the cross. When Jesus died, he took away all our sins, everything we have ever done wrong, so that we could be completely free and live our lives for him.

In the story, the servant goes free, but instead of being grateful he goes to see a fellow servant who owes him a small amount of money and demands he pay straight away and when the man can't pay he throws him into prison. The master is very angry with him and says, "I cancelled that huge debt of yours, shouldn't you now show mercy to your fellow servant?"

What Jesus is saying to us is that God has cancelled our debt of sin - a debt we could never repay and now he wants us to show mercy to those who have sinned against us and hurt us. Every time we worship together we say the words of the Lord's Prayer - 'Forgive us our sins as we forgive those who sin against us.' Jesus is asking us to forgive those who have hurt us because forgiveness pours oil onto the wounds and the effects of sin and brings healing. It brings down walls and barriers between people and is the way to understanding and peace.

So how do we forgive?
By not keeping a record of wrongs that we keep going back to or seeking revenge.
By praying for the person who has hurt us.
By being merciful towards the weaknesses of others as God is merciful to us.

Prayers

As we come to our time of prayer, let us thank God for his generous love and mercy to us all.

Heavenly Father, we thank you for sending Jesus to this world to take away the debt of our sin. Thank you Jesus for dying on the cross, for taking away my sin and for making me free to live my life for you. Lord in your mercy……..**hear our prayer**

We think of the people who have hurt us in our lives through their words and actions. We pray Lord that you would help us to forgive them. Please make us merciful to them as you are to us. Lord in your mercy….

We pray that you would bless us, that you would bless those people we have hurt in our lives, and bless those people who have hurt us. Please take away any feelings of bitterness or regret and give us your peace. Lord in your mercy….

Give me oil in my lamp
Keep me burning

Welcome and Introduction

Opening Response:

Leader:	In our watching
	In our waiting
All:	**God is alive in us**

Leader:	In our hoping
	In our praying
All:	**God is alive in us**

Leader:	In our journeying
	In our homecoming
All:	**God is alive in us**

Hymn: O Jesus I have promised

Let us confess our sin:

Leader:	Lord forgive us
All:	**Lord forgive us and help us.**

For the times we have forgotten to love you and give you thanks for all your goodness.
Lord forgive us….

For the times we have been unkind or forgotten to love those around us.
Lord forgive us…..

Lord forgive us and help us to love you and our neighbours that we might grow together as a community of love and faith.
Amen

Reading: Matt 25: 1-13

Talk

Hymn: Give me joy in my heart

Prayers
Leader: Lord in your mercy
All: **Hear our prayer**

Let us draw all these prayers together in the words of
The Lord's Prayer

All: **Our Father who art in Heaven……**

Hymn: Blessed assurance

Blessing: Wait for the Lord
                 His day is near
                 Wait for the Lord
                 Keep watch, take heart
                 and may God bless us and keep us safe
                 in the palm of his hand. **Amen.**

All: **The Grace**

Talk

The reading today is one of the stories Jesus told. Jesus often told stories as a way of explaining to the people what God is like, or to help them to understand something about God's kingdom. But sometimes his stories were difficult to understand, and his disciples were not always sure what he was getting at. It is the same for us today. So, this story is about some bridesmaids who were all ready and waiting for a wedding feast. It was their job to wait for the arrival of the bridegroom. They were supposed to wait with their oil lamps lit and burning ready welcome him. In this story it seems that the bridegroom was delayed. In our culture it is usually the bride who is late, and the poor bridegroom is waiting at the altar hoping that his bride has not changed her mind at the last minute. But in this culture, everyone is waiting for the bridegroom. It got very, very late and the bridesmaids had got a bit sleepy. But suddenly at midnight the cry rang out – he is here! The bridegroom is here! Wake up everybody!

Of course, with all that waiting the lamps had gone out, but 5 of the bridesmaids had come with some extra oil and they trimmed the lamps and got them going again and were all ready when the bridegroom arrived. They were invited into the wedding banquet together.
But sadly, there were 5 bridesmaids who hadn't come prepared with extra oil and when they hear the cry that the bridegroom is here, they have to go off to buy some more. I expect there weren't any shops open at midnight and when they get back, they find the door is already closed.

I wonder what the meaning is behind this story? What is Jesus saying to us? It is a story about keeping lamps burning right to the end.

Next week is the beginning of the season called Advent. It is the season just before Christmas. A time of Advent calendars and candles. It is the time when we are waiting for the coming of Jesus. This story about the bridesmaids is all about the coming of Jesus who is the bridegroom in this story. What he is saying to us is that he is coming. It might seem to us that he is delayed like the bridegroom in the story. I'm sure when it got to midnight some of the guests had given up hope and thought he won't come now it's much too late. But this story tells us to not give up hope. It urges us to prepare ourselves and to be ready, to keep our lamps burning brightly right to the end.

So, what does it mean to have our lamps burning? It means keeping going. Being ready to welcome Jesus into our lives. Make sure that we are right with him. Keep thinking about him. Keep praying. Keep meeting together to worship him. Keep living in hope that he is coming for us, to take us into the Heavenly banquet when the time is right for us.

Song: Give me oil in my lamp

Prayers:

As we come to our time of prayer, let us come with anticipation, with excitement and with hope that Jesus is coming and let us prepare our hearts to welcome him.

Lord Jesus as we approach the season of Advent help us to be ready to open our hearts to welcome you. Lord in your mercy.....

We pray that we would be especially aware of your presence with us here. Please fill us all with a great sense of hope and longing for you. Lord in your mercy......

We pray for all our neighbours, friends and loved ones that they would all be blessed and filled with hope. Lord in your mercy......

We pray for all who care for us here- for staff, managers and volunteers that they would be filled with strength and with your tender love and be blessed in their work. Lord in your mercy.....

The Lord's Prayer

Resources for Worship

Hymn Books

'Hymns we've always loved' - published by Kevin Mayhew
69 well known hymns and Christmas carols
Light weight paper back with large print
Accompanying 3CD box set – useful if you do not have live musical accompaniment

www.kevinmayhew.com
email: info@kevinmayhewltd.com
Tel: 01449737978

Songs of Fellowship Book 1/ Mission Praise Volume 1

Has many songs from the 1970/80's era. Residents who attended church during that era often have these songs in their memories. These songs often have simple melodies and words and are easy to sing. They can be copied in large print for residents.

Songs from the Taize Community

These songs are very simple and repetitive, often a line of scripture or simple prayer. They can be used effectively to create a prayerful mood e.g. for Remembrance, Good Friday, Advent.

Service Preparation

Seasonal services
Books by Ruth Burgess e.g.

Candles and Conifers	Advent to Christmas
Hay and Stardust	Christmas to Candlemas
Eggs and Ashes	Lent to Easter
Fire and Bread	Easter to Pentecost

Ideas for opening and closing responses, scripture readings, blessings, poems etc.

Wild Goose Publications
www.ionabooks.com

Sensory and creative worship
Books by Sue Wallace

Multi - Sensory Church
Multi - Sensory Scriptures
Multi - Sensory Prayer
Scripture Union
www.scriptureunion.org.uk

Creative Ideas for Ministry with the Aged by Sue Pickering
Canterbury Press
www.canterburypress.co.uk

Pictures

There are a wealth of visual resources produced by The Benedictine Nuns of Turvey Abbey which can be viewed on the McCrimmons website: www.mccrimmons.co.uk

Particularly recommended for use in residential care homes are the poster sets depicting Jesus in the gospels.

Jesus, Our Light	11 posters depicting the early life of Jesus - including the nativity narratives.
Jesus, Our Hope	12 posters depicting the ministry of Jesus - including some parables, healings and encounters with Jesus.
Jesus, Our Way	12 posters depicting the final events of Jesus' life including the Last Supper, the Resurrection narratives.

Posters can be purchased as sets or individually and are stocked by St. Paul's Media stores.

You Tube Videos

There are a wealth of music and visual resources which can be found on You Tube which can be used to create the right kind of mood and atmosphere for worship. Here are some examples of videos we have used very successfully.

Christmas
Sainsbury's Silent Night Christmas Advert 2014
'O Holy Night' by Josh Groben with video from 'The Nativity Story'

Christingle by Fr Simon Rundell
This video can be shown during a Christingle making activity or at the beginning of a Christingle service.

Harvest or services about meeting God in his creation
Wonderful world by Louis Armstrong
With a video by Gabrielle Marie

Remembrance
We will remember by Mike Stanley CJM
A beautiful moving video to lead into Remembrance prayers

BBC two minutes silence with Last Post

Acknowledgements

People we'd like to thank...

We want to thank the wonderful chaplains and volunteers who serve in residential care homes as part of The Gift of Years Rugby. Thank you for using the materials in this book in your services and for your commitment to creating worship that is accessible, colourful, beautiful, stimulating and filled with life. Thank you too for your helpful feedback, advice, suggestions and ideas which have helped create a resource that can be used more widely than our own context.

Thanks to our many colleagues, families and friends who have supported us in our roles.

Sources of reproduced materials

We thank the following copyright holders for giving us permission to use their materials.

Images by The Benedictine Sisters of Turvey Abbey, Used with the permission of McCrimmon Publishing Co. Ltd, Great Wakering, Essex SS3 0EQ. These wonderful images have been such an inspiration and so helpful to our residents in their understanding of the themes of the services.

Opening responses by Ruth Burgess and the Iona Community from her books; Candles and Conifers, Eggs and Ashes and Fire and Bread. Used with permission. Wild Goose Publications. www.ionabooks.com

All Scripture quotations, unless otherwise indicated, are taken from the Holy Bible, New International Version®, NIV®. Copyright ©1973, 1978, 1984, 2011 by Biblica, Inc.® Used by permission of Zondervan. All rights reserved worldwide. www.zondervan.com The "NIV" and "New International Version" are trademarks registered in the United States Patent and Trademark Office by Biblica, Inc.®

May the light of Christ music by John Howes (p12). Used with permission

Wait for the Lord (p46&47) and Jesus remember me (p120) words by J.Berthier
(c)Ateliers et Presses de Taizé, France. Used with permission

Blessing (p70) taken from Common worship: Pastoral services p378 (82) Material from Common Worship: Services and Prayers for the Church of England is copyright © 2000 The Archbishops' Council and is used here with permission.

Christ be beside me by J. Quinn (p80)

Prayer over the palms (p104) taken from The Methodist Worship Book p 237

Spirit of the Living God (p150) by Daniel Iverson (Moody Institute)

Blessing (p150) by Fr. Patrick Sayles taken from 'Lord inflame our hearts with your Spirit' page 85)used with

Blessing (p156) by Fr. Patrick Sayles taken from 'Lord inflame our hearts with your Spirit' page 88) permission

Harvest poem (p167) by Susan Wagstaff used with permission

Opening responses (p175) by David Adam taken from Daily Dedication in'The Glory of Light' SPCK

Blessing (p180) by David Adam taken from 'The Glory of Light' SPCK

God will make a way' (p229) words by Don Moen (Integrity Music used with permission)

The authors have made every effort to contact the copyright owners of all songs, prayers, blessings and illustrations. Where they have been unsuccessful they invite copyright holders to contact them directly.

Training resources by the same authors

A Life Worth Living:

The Spiritual and Social Care of Older People and People with Dementia in Residential Care.

This eight-session training course prepares chaplains, clergy, pastoral visitors, worship leaders and other volunteers to serve in care home environments with residents with complex needs and dementia.

Course Content

Session 1: Exploring the meaning of life in a care home and what does the church have to offer.

Session 2: Listening to the story - the care home context and the events that have led to a person coming to live in a care home.

Session 3: Understanding and working with people with disabilities

Session 4: Understanding and working with people with dementia

Session 5: Worshipping in a care home

Session 6: Pastoral care of older people, relatives and staff

Session 7: Part 1: Spiritual Care at the End of Life
            Part 2: Keeping ourselves and others safe (Safeguarding)

Session 8: Getting started

This course includes learners' manuals with chapters to read, group work exercises and discussions, recommended video clips, space to write notes as well as Biblical reflections to help learners to think about the work in the light of their faith.
Also available are Trainers manuals with extra pages of notes for trainers and all the resources needed to run this course.

For more information about the course and to purchase the manuals, please visit The Gift of Years website: www.thegiftofyearsrugby.com or email or telephone the authors.
Email: giftofyearsrugby@outlook.com   Tel: 07842993847

Ingram Content Group UK Ltd.
Milton Keynes UK
UKHW050846170523
421886UK00005B/9